# UPON a WISHING MOON

# UPON a WISHING MOON

DENNIS SADDLEMAN
ANTOINE MOUNTAIN
DORENE BERNARD
EUGENE ARCAND
KEITH CHIEFMOON
EVERETT SOOP

FOREWORD BY STEPHANIE SCOTT

DURVILE & UpRoute
Durvile.com

Calgary, Alberta, Canada

DURVILE.COM

DURVILE & UpRoute

UPROUTE IMPRINT OF DURVILE PUBLICATIONS LTD.
Calgary, Alberta, Canada
DURVILE.COM



LIBRARY AND ARCHIVES CATALOGUING IN PUBLICATIONS DATA

Upon a Wishing Moon: Stories, Poems, and Images by Members of the Survivors Circle of the National Centre for Truth and Reconciliation

Saddleman, Dennis, author; Mountain, Antoine, author and illustrator
Bernard, Dorene, author; Arcand, Eugene, author
Chiefmoon, Keith, author; Soop, Everett, author and illustrator
Scott, Stephanie, foreword; Laforme, R. Stacey, afterword

1. Indigenous Peoples | 2. Residential Schools
3. Canadian non-fiction | 4. Poetry | 5. Memoir

The Indigenous Spirit Series
Series editors: Crystal Many Fingers and Lorene Shyba
ISBN: 978-1-997848-14-1 (pbk) | 978-1-997848-17-2 (ebook)
978-1-997848-16-5 (audio)

Cover paintings, Antoine Mountain | Book and jacket design, Lorene Shyba

"My Life in Hockey" was adapted from "781: A Story of Sports and Survival," produced by Bob MacKenzie for The Sports Network (TSN).

The writings and artwork of Everett Soop are reproduced with the permission of Alex and Patricia Soop and the Soop family.

Durvile Publications acknowledges the financial support of the Government of Canada through the Canada Book Fund, and the Government of Alberta through the Alberta Media Fund.

Canada Alberta Government CERTIFIED CANADIAN PUBLISHER

Printed in Canada. First printing, 2026.

We are committed to protecting our natural environment. This book is made of material from well-managed FSC®-certified forests and other controlled sources.

We acknowledge the Traditional Land of the Treaty 7 Peoples of Southern Alberta. The Siksika, Piikani, and Kainai of the Blackfoot Confederacy; the Tsuut'ina Nation; and the Goodstoney, Chiniki, and Bearspaw First Nations of the Stoney Nakoda. Also, the Otipemisiwak Métis Government / Métis Nation within Alberta.

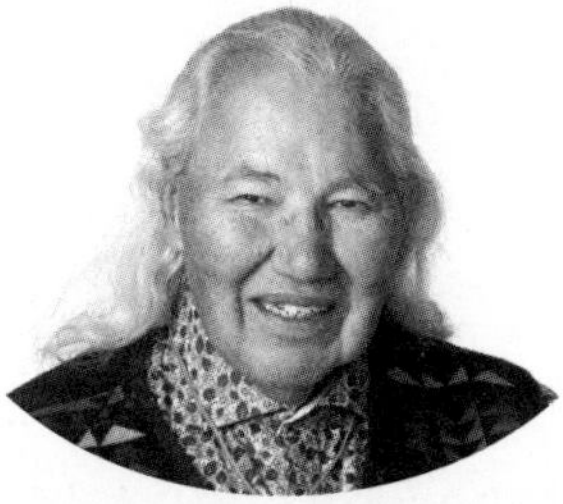

We dedicate this collection to the memory of
Mazina Giizhik-iban,
The Honourable Justice Murray Sinclair,
Anishinaabe judge, teacher, and Chair of the
Truth and Reconciliation Commission of Canada,
whose voice helped bring the
truths of Survivors
into the heart of the nation.

PHOTO: IAN MCCAUSLAND

# UPON A WISHING MOON
## CONTENTS



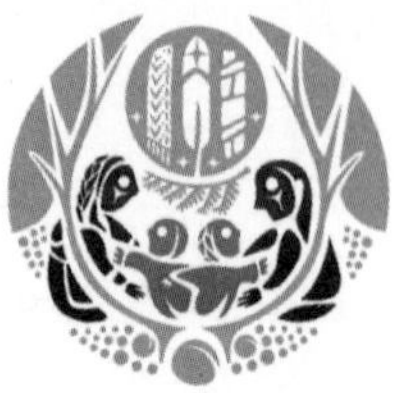



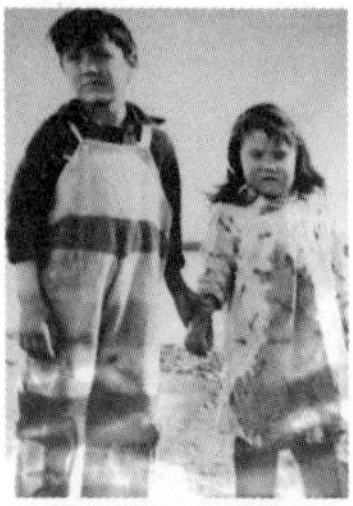

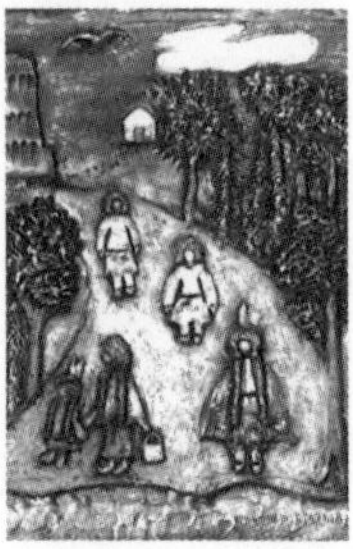

# UPON A WISHING MOON

## CONTENTS



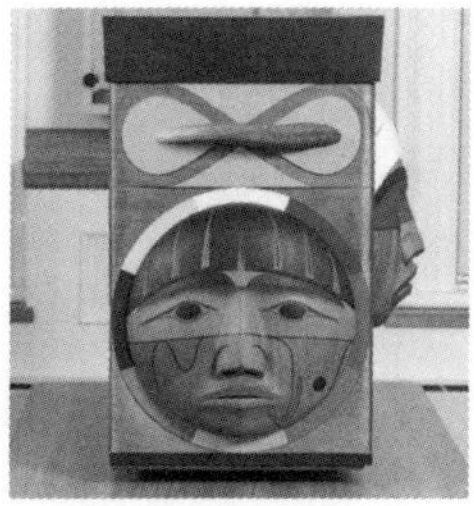

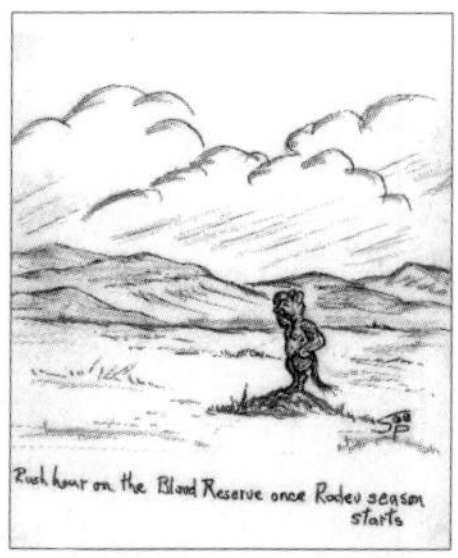


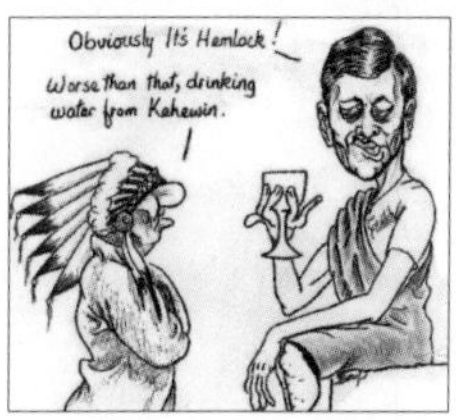

## THE SURVIVORS' FLAG

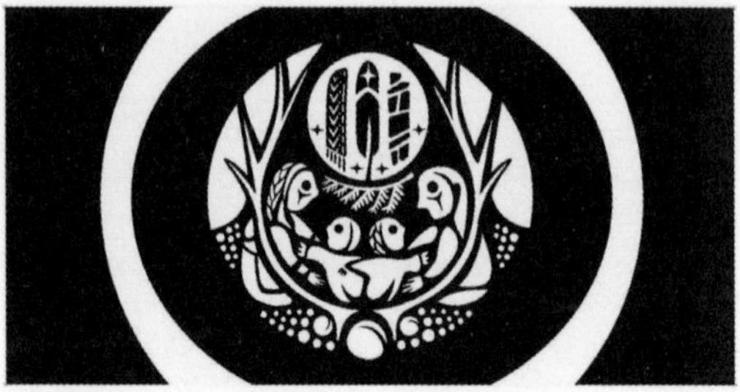

The Survivors' Flag is an expression of remembrance, meant to honour residential school Survivors and all the lives and communities impacted by the residential school system in Canada. Each element was carefully selected by Survivors from across Canada, who were consulted in the flag's creation.

### SURVIVORS WHO CONTRIBUTED TO THE FLAG'S CONCEPT AND DESIGN

Anawak, Jack — Chesterfield Inlet
Angeconeb, Garnet — Pelican IRS
Arcand, Eugene — St. Michael's IRS
Basile, Madeleine — Pointe Bleue IRS
Bernard, Dorene — Shubenacadie IRS
Bomberry, Sherlene — Mohawk Institute
Brown, Levina — Chesterfield Inlet
Brown, Terri — Yukon Hall/Coudert Residence
Bruyere, Lila — St. Margaret's IRS
Carrier, Andrew — St. Boniface Industrial School
Durocher, Jimmy — Île-à-la-Crosse Boarding School
Elias, Edna — Stringer Hall
Evaluardjuk-Palmer, Tagaaq — Churchill IRS
Felix, AJ — St. Michael's IRS
Genaille, Sylvia — Various Schools
Googoo, Phyllis — Shubenacadie IRS
Hill, Dawn — Mohawk Institute
Hill, Roberta — Mohawk Institute
Kistabish, Richard — Amos (Saint-Marc-de-Figuery) IRS
Lightning, Richard — Ermineskin (Hobbema) IRS
Longclaws, Janet — Brandon IRS
Mandamin, Roberta — Cecilia Jeffrey
Marshall Sr., Albert D. — Shubenacadie IRS
Pangborn, Irma — Camperville IRS/Assiniboia
Paynter, Florence — Sandy Bay IRS
Paynter, Philip — Sandy Bay IRS
Steinhauer, Arthur — Blue Quills IRS
Wakita, Wanbdi — Birtle IRS
Webstad, Phyllis — St. Joseph Mission (SJM) IRS
Williams, Barney — Christie IRS

## ELEMENTS OF THE FLAG

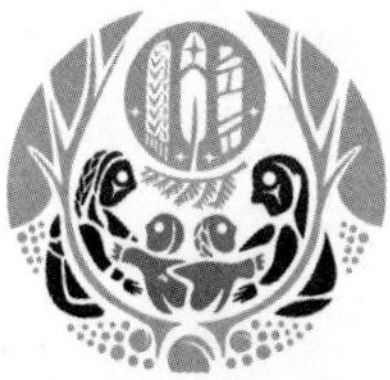

**THE FAMILY**

Some saw the adults as our ancestors watching over us; others saw these as parents signifying whole families ripped apart and also reuniting to represent healing.

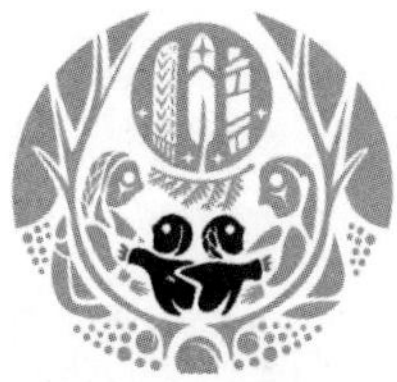

**THE CHILDREN**

More than one child is depicted in the design as often whole sibling groups were taken from their parents, younger siblings, grandparents, and community.

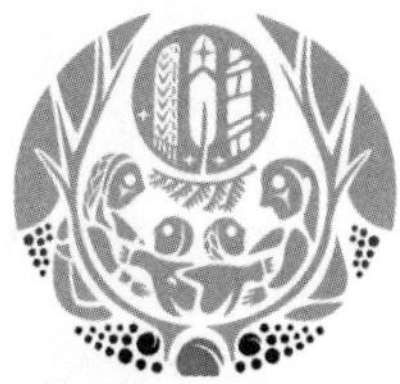

**SEEDS BELOW GROUND**

The Seeds Below Ground Represent the spirits of the children who never returned home. Although they have always been present, they are now seen and searched for.

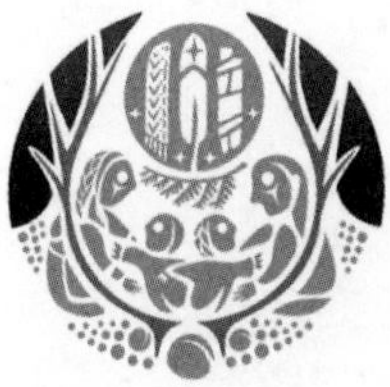

**TREE OF PEACE**

Haudenosaunee symbol of how Nations were united and brought to peace, which in turn, provides protection, comfort and renewal.

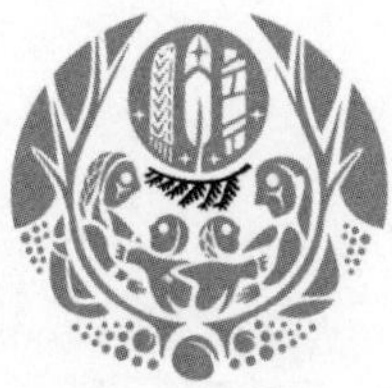

**CEDAR BRANCH**

Sacred medicine that represents protection and healing, but also what is used by some Indigenous cultures when one enters the physical world and then again when they pass on to the next. The seven branches acknowledges the seven sacred teachings taught in many Indigenous cultures.

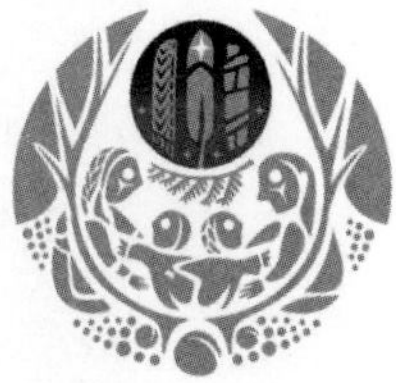

**COSMIC SYMBOLISM**

Cosmic Symbolism Represents Sun, Moon, Stars and Planets. The Sun represents the divine protection that ensure those who survived came home. The North Star is prominent as it is an important navigation guide for many Indigenous cultures.

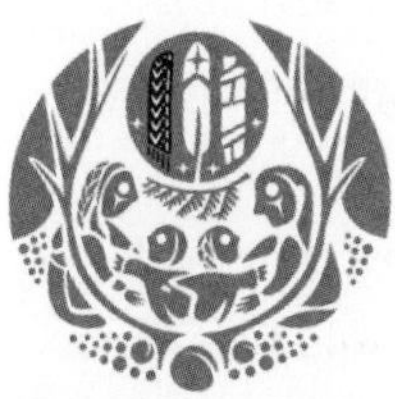

**THE MÉTIS SASH**

Certain colours of thread in the Sash represent lives that were lost, while others signal connectedness as humans and resilience through trauma. All the threads woven together spell out part of history, but no single thread defines the whole story.

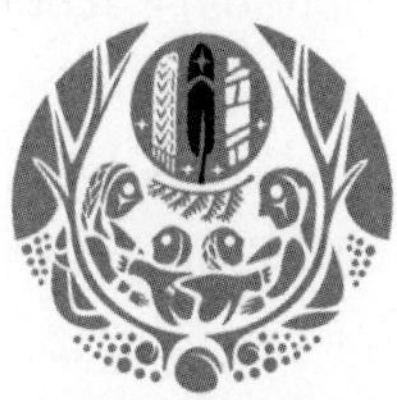

**THE EAGLE FEATHER**

The Eagle Feather represents that the Creator's spirit is among us. It is depicting pointing upwards which mirrors how it is held when one speaks their Truth.

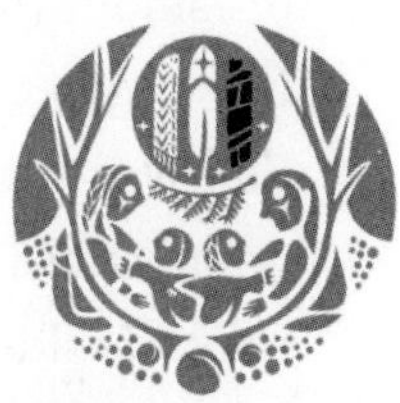

**THE INUKSUIT**

Inuksuit are used as navigational guides for Inuit people and link to tradition.

FROM WEBSITE OF
THE NATIONAL CENTRE OF
TRUTH AND RECONCILIATION
NCTR.CA

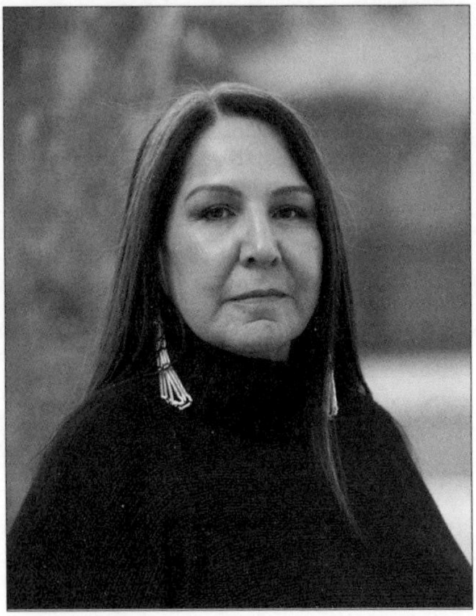

## STEPHANIE SCOTT

Stephanie Scott is the Executive Director of the National Centre for Truth and Reconciliation (NCTR) and the Associate Vice President (Indigenous) Reconciliation at the University of Manitoba. An intergenerational Survivor and Sixties Scoop Survivor, she is deeply passionate about revealing the truth about residential schools. Stephanie was born and raised in Winnipeg and her maternal family hails from Roseau River Anishinabe First Nation, Treaty One Territory.

*Foreword*

# THE POWER OF TRUTH
## STEPHANIE SCOTT

ANY TIME that a Survivor of Canada's Indian Residential School system shares their truths, they are giving us an extraordinary gift.

In this collection, six residential school Survivors powerfully express their truths in the form of poems, drawings, photographs, memoirs, and sacred teachings. In their own distinctive ways, they are giving voice to all the young ones who were torn away from loving families to endure unimaginable abuse at the hands of church and state. They are candidly illustrating the long, and still unfinished journeys to heal from this profound individual and collective trauma. And, perhaps more than anything else, they are demonstrating that despite the terrible harm done by the residential schools, First Nations, Inuit, and Métis cultures and traditions are still alive, vibrant, and strong.

In one of his pieces in this collection, "A Friend for Life," Dr. Antoine Mountain tells us not only about his lifelong friend, Roy Goose, but also that the fireweed, the first plant to bloom after a wildfire, is "our sign for hope." The truths shared in this collection are like the fireweed. Yes, they remind us of the terrible history that has ravaged our Nations. However, they are also signs of hope, a demonstration that our Nations are deeply rooted in these lands and are ready to flourish again.

The authors of this book were among more than 150,000 First Nations, Inuit, and Métis children who were taken from their families during the 150 years of Canada's Indian Residential School system. As their stories attest, abuse and neglect were widespread at these schools. The food was poor. The dorms were overcrowded. Contagious diseases were rampant. There was physical and sexual abuse. Neglect. And none of this was by accident.

Between 2008 and 2015, the Truth and Reconciliation Commission of Canada (TRC) travelled throughout Canada, hearing from more than 6,500 residential schools Survivors and other eyewitnesses. The TRC also reviewed a vast number of church and government documents, many of which had never been made public. In its final report, the TRC sets out its clear and inescapable conclusion that residential schools were part of "a systematic, government-sponsored attempt to destroy Aboriginal cultures and languages."

This was the context in which the residential schools were created and run. This is why widespread reports of violent punishments, malnutrition, and sickness were ignored. This is why staff got away with abusing young children. And this is why, for decades, Survivors who have tried to talk about their experiences were met with hostility and denial.

Today, we are fortunate to have the opportunity to read honest accounts of Survivors' experiences in books like this one. That wasn't always the case.

The TRC. The Indian Residential School Settlement Agreement. Canada's Apology. These things were made possible by decades of struggle by Survivors who insisted that their truths be heard. Survivors who took the government and churches to court. Survivors who forced Canada to acknowledge what had happened to them — and why.

Many of the writers and artists featured in this collection talk about how hard it has been to tell their own stories. About feeling ashamed over the abuse they had endured. About struggling to find the words to express their trauma and loss.

In one of his poems featured in this collection, Dennis Saddleman talks about how the very words "residential school" reopen old wounds. Yet despite this, Dennis has found the strength and motivation to write, saying, "The words Residential School, they were afraid of one word, Truth."

Survivors have demonstrated extraordinary courage and persistence in telling their truths. This is a gift that we should all honour. As Eugene Arcand describes, the National Centre for Truth and Reconciliation (NCTR) was specifically created to carry on the work begun by the

TRC. We are the respectful steward for Survivors' statements and millions of other records that document the history of the residential school system. On this foundation, we continue to carry out research so that the full story can be told. We also engage with Canadians of all ages through public education programs to ensure that these truths are never forgotten.

The NCTR was created with a vital national mandate. But we were created without guaranteed funding and without a permanent home, and we have operated out of a temporary facility on the University of Manitoba campus — an old brick house, which we have long outgrown. With seed funding from the federal government, and land offered by the university as an act of truth and reconciliation, the realization of our vision for a new home is growing ever closer to becoming a reality. Building a new home for the NCTR is a once-in-a-lifetime national legacy project.

In all this work, the NCTR is guided by a Survivors Circle, comprised of First Nations, Inuit, and Métis Survivors from across Turtle Island, many of whom contributed to this collection. Their leadership, and their involvement in every aspect of our work, ensures that Survivors' voices are always respected and heard.

Of course, the contributions made by Survivors go far beyond the NCTR. The inclusion of the late Everett Soop's cartoons from the early 1980s reminds us that Survivors have not only preserved our cultures and traditions, they have also been at the forefront of the contemporary resurgence in Indigenous languages, identity, and pride.

As Keith Chiefmoon, Ga'na (kainai) Sundance teacher and Blackfoot language holder writes, despite the ravages of the residential school system, the languages, the teachings and the laws that define our cultures and traditions have not been lost.

> They are still there. Our parents carried them. The land still carries them. The stars still carry them. It takes time to come back to that. To remember who you are. To live those teachings again. That is what we are doing now.

I have had the pleasure to get to know the authors and artists featured in this collection through their roles as members of the NCTR's Survivors Circle and Governing Circle. I know them as friends and teachers. As leaders and mentors. I am very happy that through this book, others will also get to know them, to learn from their wisdom, and to be inspired by their examples.

Survivors have done more than just survived residential schools — they are living in their power and have given so much to our country as artists, poets, language holders, ceremonial keepers, and as leaders in fields such as medicine, law, and politics.

In her chapter, Dorene Bernard writes, "You will have many Elders' Teachings during your lifetime, as I have, and there will be those that you embrace, practice, and share with others."

Each of the Survivors included in this collection — Dennis, Dorene, Antoine, Keith, Eugene, and Everett — have given us a great gift. To borrow Doreen's words, "My hope is that you will embrace this gift, practice what you learned, and share this gift with others in the same generosity of heart and spirit with which it has been offered."

• • •

When the NCTR was established, Survivors envisioned a place where the truths of their residential school experiences would be honoured and preserved for future generations. With a founding contribution of $60 million from the federal government, the NCTR and the University of Manitoba launched a fundraising campaign to secure the remaining funds needed for its permanent home.

This new home will serve as an international learning lodge where Survivors, their families, and people from Canada and around the world can learn about the history and legacy of Indian residential schools. More than a building, it will be a permanent gathering place for learning, remembrance, celebration, and truth, guided by the vision of Survivors.

— *Stephanie Scott, Executive Director*
*The National Centre for Truth and*
*Reconciliation, Winnipeg, Manitoba, 2026*

# THE AUTHORS

Dennis Saddleman

Dr. Antoine Mountain

Dorene Bernard

Eugene Arcand

Keith Chiefmoon

Everett Soop

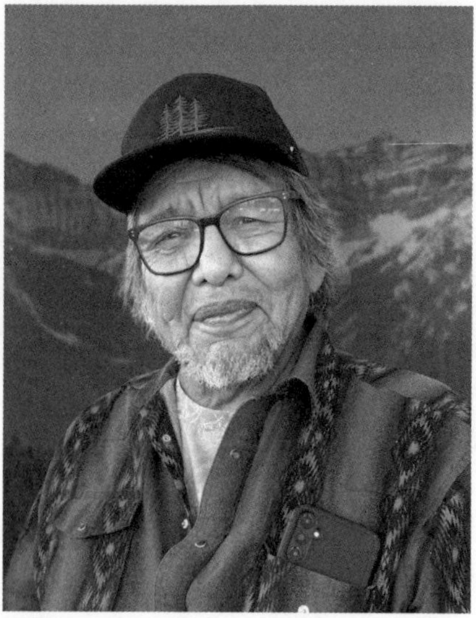

PHOTO: LORENE SHYBA

## DENNIS SADDLEMAN

Dennis Saddleman is Nlaka'pamux on his mother's side and Syilx on his father's. He attended Kamloops Indian Residential School for 11 years. After enduring profound loss, addiction, and hardship, he began a lifelong healing journey. Now 46 years sober, he shares his story and poetry widely. His work has gained international recognition. Known as "Word Warrior," he carries forward the strength and voice of his ancestors.

## Upon a Wishing Moon

Step outside.
Walk into the night.
Feet on the ground.
Look up. Look way up.
It's dark. It's cloudy. Nothing to see.
You are a child. Imaginations run wild.
Indeed, you're a child of the moon.
Transformed into Moonchild.
Moonchild. Wonderer of the night sky.
Wonderer of people's dreams.
Moonchild you're drawn to the universe.
Footprints never fade.
Frolicking with Night child.
And with glee and joy, you bounced
    from star to star.
It's another night.
Step outside.
Walk into the night.
Feet on the ground.
Look up. Look way up.
It's dark. It's cloudy. Nothing to see.
A story, a sad story of long ago.
A child. A child of long ago.
A lonely child far away from home.
A child, he was behind closed doors.
A child, in a big room. A child, in a little bed.
Oh! This lonely place. This lonely place.
No mommy! No daddy to say I love you.

No mommy! No daddy to hug you.
The child cried. He cried and cried.
His tears wet the pillow.
He crawled out of bed. He went to the window sill.
His snotty nose on the window glass.
He saw the moon hanging in the sky.
Oh moon! Do you see my home?
My home far away. My home beyond my reach.
My home beyond the mountains.
Oh moon! Do you see my mommy and daddy?
My mommy and daddy so far away.
The moon said nothing.
All it did was hang in the sky. Hang in the sky.
The child, he felt sad. He went back to bed.
Back to bed and cried all night. Cried all night.
Another night gone.
Another night came.
Step outside.
Walk into the night.
Feet on the ground.
Look up. Look way up.
It's dark. It's cloudy. Nothing to see.
The day is ending.
I'm afraid of the night.
Afraid of darkness.
Afraid of the shadows.
Afraid the night creatures would get me.
I rely upon her courage.
    I surrendered myself to her beauty.

High above the sky. She danced with my soul
To me she's full of life. She's the full moon.
She has full breasts. She has full breasts.
    I can sleep on, I can dream on.

**Sweety!**

You're my sweetness, a flame to my heart.
There were a million flowers out there,
    I picked you the most beautiful one.
There was a million stars in the universe,
    I picked you the shiniest one.
The moment I met you, there were a million moments
    that became forever and ever.
Time knew my needs. It's now or never.
Our eyes met. The word lonely packed up and went away.
I wasn't a perfect man but our love together
    made us perfect.
We were perfect in the presence of the Creator.
We were perfect to sacredness.
Our wedding rings blessed by our love.
At the alter in the presence of our family and friends.
Our vows connected us. We held hands.
Devotions will live with us.
Faith will live with us.
The moon and the stars, they will keep us romantic.
Together in the presence of our memories.
In the presences of our responsibilities.
We will walk beyond and remember our vows
    wrapped around our fingers.

## Existence with Purpose

Existence that surrounded me.
There be existence that woke up every day.
There be existence in my childhood.
In my veins. In my dreams.
My soul, my soul with no age.
My soul that walked in fantasies and in reality.
My soul with my name.
My name written on the first day
    and the last day on Earth.
My identity flowing in the veins of
    my grandmother and grandfather.
There are deep scars I wore
    like war paint on my face.
I represent all my struggles,
    they bless me to get up.
I represent all my mistakes
    that pursued forgiveness.
I represent determination called above and
    beyond.
I will look up and touch the sky.
I will put my life in the hands of tomorrow.
In the hands of existence, you only live once.

**Survivors**

There's a warning sign ahead. Proceed with caution.
There was a man in a black robe standing outside.
There was a monster, its flesh made of bricks.
The monster was choking and gagging.
    Choking and gagging.
It spit out a child. The monster looked at the child.
    What's that?
The man in the black robe said, "It's nothing. Don't
    worry. Throw the child in the darkness.
    Nobody cares."

There was a man in a black robe standing outside.
The monster, it had many window eyes.
The monster was choking and gagging.
    Choking and gagging.
It spit out a child. The monster looked at the child.
    What's that?
The man in the black robe said, "It's nothing.
    Don't worry. Throw the child in prison.
    Nobody cares."

There was a man in a black robe standing outside.
There was a monster, it had with two red doors.
The monster was choking and gagging.
    Choking and gagging.
It spit out a naked child. What's that?
The man in the black robe his eyes became wide.
"Cover up the child! Cover up the child.
No one must know. No one must know!"

There was a man in a black robe standing outside
The monster was choking and gagging.
    Choking and gagging.
The monster threw up on the ground.
The man in the black robe walked away
    and disappeared.
The monster cried and cried.
    He said, "I don't want to be a monster anymore.
    Nobody likes me. Nobody likes me."

A child came out darkness. He wore a smile.
    The child walked into the light.
    The child spoke to the Monster.
    "I like you. I think you're a good monster."
The monster argued. "No! No! No! I'm a horrible
    monster. I ate some children."
A child returned from prison. The child spoke to
    the Monster. "I like you. I think you're a won-
    derful monster."
The monster kept arguing.
    "No! No! No! I'm a terrible Monster.
I ate everything you owned."

A naked child appeared. In his arms he had folded
    clothes. He put on his clothes.
    He spoke to the Monster. "I like you. I think
    you're an awesome Monster."
The monster trembled. The monster cried, "But I
    threw you in darkness. I threw you in prison.
    I threw your clothes away."

The three children stood together. One of them spoke:
"Starve the Monster. Starve the Monster.
Make the Monster hungry.
Feed the Monster love.
Feed the Monster forgiveness.
Feed the Monster a big bowl of Alphabits
that spell gentle and kind."

**How Do You Bloom?**

You can bloom anywhere, anytime.
How do you bloom?
I wish I was every flower, everywhere.
I wish I was every beautiful flower.
How do you bloom?
Mother Earth, she embraced me.
Embraced the seed.
The power of emergence reached out.
Pulled me out of the ground.
I felt Father Sun, he touched me.
And I grew and grew and grew.
How do you bloom?
Every day and tomorrow,
I will plant my feet in my shoes and I will bloom.
I will bloom on the side of every path,
on the side of every road.
I will bloom in the garden of my destinations.
How do you bloom?
Remove all the bad weeds and pour water of life
unto knowledge and wisdom.

Walk with the young ones, walk with the Elders.
You will bloom and they will blossom.
Do not step on the ants, do not be afraid
    to flow into the ocean.
You will bloom and they will blossom.
You and the thousands of flowers in the community,
    an emblem of beauty and hope.
You and the thousands of flowers in the community,
    cast your shadows over the weeds.

**We All Need a Friend**

Happiness was jumping with the child.
Happiness was playing with the child.
Without warning a swift hand appeared.
Whack! On the side of the head.
The child fell on the cement floor.
An angry voice shook the child.
YOU CANNOT BE HAPPY HERE!
Sadness came and helped the child to his feet.
Laughter was laughing and laughing with child.
Laughter was having fun with the child.
Without warning a swift hand appeared.
Whack! On the side of the head.
The child fell on the cement floor.
An angry voice shook the child.
NO LAUGHING HERE!
Tears came and helped the child to his feet.
Love ran up to the child. Love hugged the child.
Without warning a swift hand appeared.

Whack! On the side of the head.
The child fell on the cement floor.
An angry voice shook the child.
IN HERE THERE'S NO SUCH THING AS LOVE.
When no one was looking.
A friend came.
A friend said hello to the child.
A friend helped the child to his feet.
A friend gave the child a piece of bread.

**Dreaming Where I Fell**

I was dreaming where I fell.
Stumbled.
Tumbled.
Went through the air.
Went towards the ground.
Mighty impact.
Cracked my emotions.
The snow fell.
The rain fell.
A tree fell.
Even love fell.
I was dreaming where I fell.
Dizzy.
Confused.
Rattled.
I went to the edge of the world.
I slipped, I fell and fell and fell.
My dream didn't stop.

I fell and fell and fell.
I drank forbidden wine, I fell.
The moonlight kissed me, I fell.
The candle went out, I fell.
Hunger struck me, I fell.
I tried to keep my balance.
My balance wasn't there.
Divided and conquered, I fell.
I had a broken wing, I fell.
I followed a star, I fell.
I fell and fell and fell.
I tried to grab something, I fell.
When the sun went down, I fell.
I think my dream will continue another night.
Another night. Another night.

**Residential School**

This pen didn't want to write.
I scribbled on a page.
My scribbling didn't make sense.
The next page, it was blank
I sat there. I sat there.
If I wrote the words: Residential School.
My writing hand would tremble.
My forehead, it would drip with sweat.
I turned the page to write.
My breathing erratic.
I wished my pen didn't have any ink.
I wanted to tear out the page and crumple it with anger.

I wanted to close the book and never begin.
The words Residential School kept gnawing
my soul.
I was afraid the words Residential School, they would
cut my veins and all the ancestors will vanish.
I was afraid the words Residential School, they would
take my childhood and vanish forever.
I squeezed the pen, hoping it would break.
The words Residential School sneered at me.
"I'm going to sneak into the next generation and
the next generation and steal their hopes and
dreams."
I bit my lip. With a shaky hand, I wrote the words
Residential School.
My writing was chicken scratch. The words
Residential School, they surrendered to my stories.
The words Residential School, they were afraid of
one word, Truth.

**The Almighty Father and The Almighty Warrior**

They said, "The Almighty Father created the world."
I created my own world. I'm the creator of what
I built. I think about the Almighty Father and I
think about who I am, the Almighty Warrior. Do I
dare to compare myself with the Almighty Father?
I wore the eyes of the Residential School.
The eyes of the devil, the eyes of evil and sin.
The poisonous snakes of drugs and alcohol bit me.
There was thunder in my mouth.

Lightening scared my dreams and my visions,
    they ran away.
I did not know who I was. I found a paint brush.
With a paint brush from my childhood.
With a paint brush from my ancestors.
I painted my true colours.
My skin is brown.
My blood is red.
You are The Almighty Father.
I'll be The Mighty Warrior.
You live in heaven.
I live on Earth.
You perform miracles.
I'm The Aboriginal Super Hero.
You are the Spiritual Being.
I'm The Physical Being.
You carried The Cross.
I'm The Beast of Burden.
You're Unseen.
I left my tracks everywhere.
You rose.
I fell.
You walked the stairway to heaven.
I climbed mountains.
You wore a halo.
I wore a feather.
You're Heavenly
I'm Nlka'pamux.
You have angels.

I have ancestors.
You can walk on water.
I can paddle my canoe.
You're everywhere.
I'm there when someone needs me.
You're Supreme.
I'm Beautiful and Smart.
You're everything.
I'm one soul.
You're everything.
I'm one body.
You're The Almighty Father.
I'm The Mighty Warrior.

### A Residential School Morning

Some mornings the birds don't sing.
Some mornings the river flowed with sadness.
Some mornings the mountains above the school,
    they cried for the children, rocky tears rolled
    down their rocky faces.
A new day arrived. You wondered if this new day
    will be a friend or foe.
Wakefulness nudged you and you
    sat up on your bed.
You tried to look beyond the day.
It was too blurry.
Too far away.
You tried to look beyond the day.
Fear blocked your vision.

Unknown stood in your way.
You don't know if the scary leather strap
    was waiting for you.
You don't know if a backhand was waiting for you.
You don't know if a kick in the butt was
    waiting for you.
You don't know if evil and sin was waiting for you.
You don't know if a bully was waiting for you.
You don't know if you would miss a meal.
You tried to look beyond the day.
Beyond the day so far away.
If you can make it through this day, through this day.
If you can survive this one day. This one whole day.
It would be a miracle.
It would be a miracle.

**My Life as a Wino**

FOR GOD'S SAKES
    WHAT ARE YOU DOING HERE?
My stupid choice put me here.
    I never thought I would end up here.
I opened my eyes. My body was curled up.
There was sunlight.
I wondered if Father Sun was ashamed of me.
What's that stench?
Back-alley odor.
I sat up, my body was stiff.
A cardboard was my bed.
I slept beside a dumpster.

My mouth was dry and it tasted yucky.
There was puke on my coat.
I stood up.
Unsteady legs.
My stomach churning.
I heaved and heaved.
Empty wine bottle near my foot.
With shaky hands I searched my pockets.
I found a few coins and a
    crumpled up two-dollar bill.
I need more moolah for my next bottle.
Shaky hands, shaky lips
    I removed my coat and threw it away.
I went to the streets.
Hello! Hello!
Do you have any change?
Do you have any change?
Thank you! Thank you!
Have a nice day.

**Millions**

I looked at someone's face.
An old wrinkled face.
It looked like an old plow went through his brown skin.
I'm an old man from Kolewadda.
I wore the scars of the residential school.
    Deep! Deep scars.
In that dreadful school they tried
    to kill the Indian inside of me.

In that dreadful school I was
    physically abused and sexually abused.
I felt ashamed.
Shame upon shame.
My scars reminded me I'm not worthy.
Day after day went by.
Year after year went by.
A lot of thoughts came to my mind.
A lot of words became prayers.
A lot of roads led me to resiliency.
I had a million reasons to smile.
A million reasons to laugh.
Now there are millions of stars
    that tell me there's hope.
There are millions of raindrops that tell me,
    it's okay to cry.
There are millions of flowers
    that tell me I'm beautiful.
There are millions of trees
    that tell me I have family roots.
Millions of pains. Millions of wounds.
    Millions of bandages.
Yesterday and beyond,
I walked a million steps.
Tomorrow and beyond.
There will be millions of steps ahead of me.

## The Drum Goes Bang

The drum goes bang.
The bang goes everywhere.
It's time to sing.
It's time to pray.
The drum goes bang.
Bang! Bang! Bang!
Join the circle.
Sacred circle.
Bring your medicine.
Bring your spirit.
The drum goes bang.
Bang! Bang! Bang!
Bang! Bang! Bang!
Dance for me.
Dance for everyone.
Dance! Dance! Dance!
Dance! Dance! Dance!
Ruffle your feathers.
Move your moccasins.
Keep the beat.
Beat! Beat! Beat!
Beat! Beat! Beat!
Bang! Bang! Bang!
Bang! Bang! Bang!
Bang!
Bang!
BANG!

**I'm Bleeding.**

Do not look for me.
Do not write any words.
Do not write any stories.
Do not think of any titles.
Do not open the book.
Page one it's not there.
Page one it's hidden in the past.
Do not look for me.
Do not worry about me.
I'm good.
I wore a long coat of silence.
Silence had no name.
I like it that way.
Silence shrouded my identity.
Do not look my way.
I'm beneath evil.
I'm beneath sin.
Stand back!
A flashback sliced my memory.
My memory, it's bleeding!
                    Bleeding!
                    Bleeding!
My poems.
My stories it dripped!
                Dripped!
                Dripped!

## Worst Drunk

I believed I was the worst drunk in town,
because I slept in the back alleys.
I believed I was the worst drunk in my community
because I was a drunken Indian in a gutter.
I believed I was the worst drunk in my family
because booze came first, booze was the most important thing in my life.
I drank; I went down. I drank; I kept going down further and further. I drank; I was in darkness. I drank and drank. My appearance looked pitiful. I went from a young handsome man to someone staggering the streets.
My hair was long and greasy. I smelled bad. I never had a bath for weeks. I wore the same clothes for long time. I smelled like urine and puke. I often slept in the back alleys beside the dumpsters. I drank a lot of wine and I drank Lysol. I ate food from the dumpsters. I dug in my pockets hoping to find enough money for the next bottle.
If someone from my family saw me. They might say,
"For God sakes, what are you doing here?"
I stood there. I cannot look at anybody eye to eye. I made a wrong choice. First, I drank. I became a heavy drinker. I lost control. I hit bottom. I didn't know how to get up. I didn't know how to ask for help. I have nothing. I have nothing to give.

Alcohol equals nothing.
    Sobriety equals one thing for everything.
My mind, my thoughts, always about booze,
    always about wine.
My mind, my thoughts, clean out the junk and
    throw it away, throw it out the window.
Throw away the darkness. Throw away the demons.
    Throw away the shame.
I got to start somewhere. I'm at the bottom. I have
    to build, a foundation for my new life. My new
    life like a new car, it will carry me long ways.
    My new life will marry a good life. Together we
    will live in self-respect. Together we will make
    better choices. I was blessed, I was given another
    chance at life. I've been sobered for 46 years.

**The Word Beautiful, It Means Something**

Beautiful! Something to see.
Something to touch.
Something to feel.
Beautiful! A smile written on your face.
A smile kissed your soft lips.
A smile impressed another smile.
Beautiful! Wild flowers bloom for you.
Wild flowers they tell you, this land, connected to
    you, grow anywhere you want.
Beautiful! The stars talked about you.

The word beautiful, it means something.
The sun waited for the night.

The night waited for the dreams.
The songs in your heart waited to be sung.

The word beautiful, it means something.
Beautiful spirits they walked with you.
Beautiful ancestors all around you.
Beautiful ancestors always and forever.

The word beautiful it means something.
All the Residential School Survivors,
Once you were children.
You had dreams.
You had your name written on hope.
Hope, it's like a scar on tomorrow.

The word beautiful, it means something.
It means you and me,
    we're not perfect but beautiful.

**The Dancer**

Everyone dancing except you.
You're alone while everyone's dancing.
Shyness does not want to dance.
A dancer from the dance floor approached you.
The beautiful dancer smiled.
"May I have this dance?"
Hesitation pulled you back.
The music urged you.
The rhythm stirred you.
Like the sun you rose.
Like the courage of million warriors, you accepted.

The dancing floor beckoned your feet.
The music melted and seeped into your body.
It was the Creator who made you.
You were made for dancing.
The beat banged in your heart.
The motion in your body swayed back and forth.
The motion like a cobra snake.
The music became louder and louder.
It's okay to be free.
The world is yours.
You're dancing with the most beautiful dancer.
You're dancing like no one was watching.
You got the John Travolta moves.
You're all shook up like Elvis Presley.
You're graceful deer in the forest.
The ancestors stomped their feet,
    clapped their hands.
The beat.
The swirls.
The twirls.
The passion told a story.
The butterfly and a flower perfect pair for a dance.
Thunder and lightning perfect pair for a dance.
The wind and the trees perfect pair for a dance.
The music ended.
Your spirit, your inner child was breathless.
You're a dancer. A dancer.
The beautiful dancer bowed and she said,
"Thank you for this dance."

## Dear Autumn

September said,
  "I got to change, it's been a long hot summer."
End of summer said,
  "Head to the water for a final splash."
Swim in the ocean. Swim in the blue sky.
Who are you watching? Sit on a hill. Her name is
  beautiful.
She is the season in the sun
She'll harmonize you with comfort and true colours.
If I was a leaf, I would go on the autumn floor
  and dance in the wind.
Dear autumn, may your beautiful colours
  wash me and heal me.
Dear autumn, the trees are beautiful,
  they're wearing robes of gold and red.
The trees are beautiful. They're honouring the
  Residential School Survivors.
The trees are beautiful. They're honouring the
  children that didn't make it home.
The trees are beautiful. They're wearing orange
  leaves, orange leaves.
Every child matters.

**Enter the Liquor Store**

In the liquor store there were shelves upon shelves.
Booze upon booze.
Enter the liquor store, upon these shelves:
Dark spirits.
Wine spirits.
Whiskey spirits.
Poison spirits.
Enter the liquor store.
Who walked in.
A wino.
A straight whiskey drinker.
A beer guzzler, a party animal.
Enter at your own risk.
On the counter leave all your hard earnings.
On the counter your children with empty stomachs.
On the counter unpaid bills.
Broken promises, broken homes.
Exit the liquor store.
Come back anytime.
WINE NOT!!

**Fire**

A fire was struck by a match.
A fire was struck by lightning.
A fire wasn't a fire until anger raged.
A fire's dance floor is in the forest.
A fire's life: Burn! Burn! Burn out of control.
A fire's path: Burn everything in sight.

A fire can be beautiful or it can be hell.
A fire can kiss the sky.
A fire can be a demon with speed.
A fire can jump high and far.
A fire can roar.
A fire can give birth to embers and sparks.
A fire loves a cigarette butt.
A fire with or without warning you must evacuate.

### Once We Were Warriors

Once we were many.
We were taller than pride.
Our courage was our armour.
We went to the battlefield.
We fought the residential school.
We fought the federal government.
We fought the churches.
Many warriors fell.
They were killing the Indian in the child.
Many warriors cannot speak their languages.
Many warriors had their identity taken away.
Many warriors could not follow their ancestors' way.
Once we were many.
We were brave.
We stood up for our children.
We stood up for our grandchildren.
We stood up for the unborn.
We fought the residential school.
We fought the federal government.

We fought the churches.
Many warriors fell.
Darkness swallowed them.
Alcohol killed them.
Drugs took them.
Once we were many.
We were warriors.
We were courageous.
We were heroes.
The residential school.
The Federal Government.
The churches.
They tried to get rid of us.
Once we were many.
Do not forget those who are gone.
Do not forget those who are still with us.
We are warriors.
We are survivors.
Our perseverance.
Our resilience.
Made us rise.
Made us tall as the mountains.
Once we were many.

## To All the Children

I left Kamloops Residential School in 1967. I wondered
about the children I went to school with.
After residential school, hundreds of children,
hundreds of children went home.
The entrance door opened.
Hundreds of children met their freedom.
Some went that way, some went this way.
Some went over the mountain.
Some went across the river.
Some flew away.
To all the children, I never said goodbye.
To all the children, thank you for being part of my life.
To all the children, I went to school with.
I think about you often.
I wonder where you are.
I prayed for you.
Are you gone? Are you with us?
Are you hurting? Are you struggling?
Are you okay? Are you safe?
To all the children I went to school with.
I think about you.
I prayed for you.
I drummed for you.
I sang for you.
I danced for you.
To all the children I went to school with.
I sent you love and hugs
I sent you love and peace.

## One Trapped Spirit

Shhhhh! Be quiet. Do not disturb them. The nuns and priest, they chase you and they'll catch you. They want to keep your spirit, forever.
Run! Run! Run!
They're after you.
They'll catch you.
Run fast! Run quick!
Run anywhere!
Somewhere!
Run through your mind!
Run over there!
Run! Run! Run!
Run through your heart. Hurry!
Don't stumble! Don't fall!
Run up! Run down! Up and down the stairs!
Run through the dormitory!
Run through the church!
Run through the dining room!
Run through the halls!
Run! Run! Run!
Zig-zag! Dodge! Zig-zag! Dodge!
Run for the door! Run for the door!
Open the door! Open the door and run!
Run for your freedom! Run for your freedom!
Run home! Run home!
Free your spirit!
Free your spirit!
Free your spirit!

## The Pond People

In 1966 my dad chose to have our new house built by the pond.

In the pond there lived the duck people, the frog people, the otter people and the beaver people. Other side of the pond there's the highway. In winter, people can skate on the pond. In summer frogs sang during the day and during the night. My parents are gone; they took their spiritual journey many years ago. Today my wife Jean and I, we live in the house by the pond.

Look! Look at the pond!

On the water surface. Bubbles! Bubbles!

On the water surface. Something emerged. Something came out of the water. It was a man and a woman. They stood at the edge of the pond. Water dripping to the ground. They smelled like the pond. Their clothes were old and raggedy. Their flesh greenish and blueish. Together the man and the woman walked up a hill. They walked to the house. They stood at the door.

In the house there was an old man at the table eating breakfast. The old man's name, Dennis. His wife Jean was baking a chocolate cake.

There was a knock on the door. Dennis opened the door. He was surprised to see strange characters on the porch. Dennis wasn't afraid. He invited the strangers in. Told them to sit by the fire and warm up. Jean offered them coffee and cake. The visitors were happy for the kindness they received. They hugged Dennis and Jean, when that happened, Dennis and Jean became the Pond People. The visitors bid goodbye and they went back to the pond.

## A Residential School Dream

In the dream, I woke up.
I didn't move; I listened.
Somewhere I heard the door slam.
I heard voices but I couldn't make out
  what they're saying.
I heard echoing footsteps.
Slowly I sat up.
The dormitory was dark.
I got out of bed and stood up.
On the ceiling, dim lights flickered.
There were some children sleeping on their beds.
At the other end of the big room, there was
  a nun and a priest standing together.
My first thought, the children.
I must get the children out of here.
I scrambled to each bed to wake up a child.
I gathered all the children.
I looked at the nun and the priest,
  they were coming towards us.
Some children were afraid.
I moved all the children to the fire escape door.
I looked at the nun and the priest, they looked dead.
The nun and the priest they weren't walking.
They were floating about three inches
  above the floor.
I opened the door; I shooed the children out.
I looked at the nun and the priest,
  they were going to grab me

I fell backwards.
    I tumbled down the fire escape stairs.
The door closed. The door closed. And I woke up.

### Here Comes, A Lullaby

A song I sang at the talent show. I came in fourth.
Here comes daddy-da-da-da
Here come mommy-mom-mom-mom
Here comes brother-bro-bro-bro
Here comes sister-sis-sis-sis
Here comes gramma-ma-ma-ma
Here comes grampa-pa-pa-pa
Here comes uncle-unk-unk-unk
Here auntie-ant-ant-ant
Here comes the mob-buh-buh-buh
Here comes the police-lease-lease-lease
Here comes the teacher-tee-tee-tee
Here comes the students-stew-stew-stew
Here comes homework-ho-ho-ho
Here comes the clouds-clah-clah-clah
Here comes the rain-ray-ray-ray
Here comes the rainbow-bow-bow-bow
Here comes the sun-un-un-un
Here comes the moon-moo-moo-moo
Here comes the stars-are-are-are
Here comes the night-nye-nye-nye
Here comes the sleep-leap-leap-leap
Close your eyes, close your eyes and sing again.

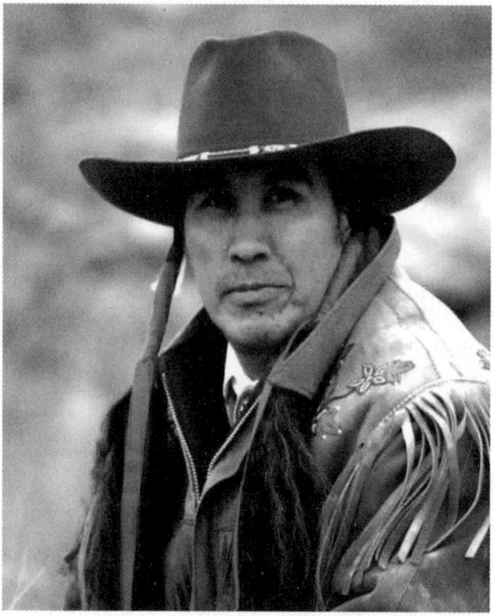

PHOTO: THIS NEXT GENERATION

## DR. ANTOINE MOUNTAIN

Antoine Mountain is a Dene artist, activist, and scholar from Radelie Koe (Fort Good Hope), Northwest Territories. Taken from his family at age nine, he was sent to three residential schools, including the notorious Grollier Hall in Inuvik, spending 12 years in the system. A member of the Survivors Circle at the National Centre for Truth and Reconciliation, he is committed to raising awareness of intergenerational trauma and helping youth understand its lasting impacts.

## Somewhere Else

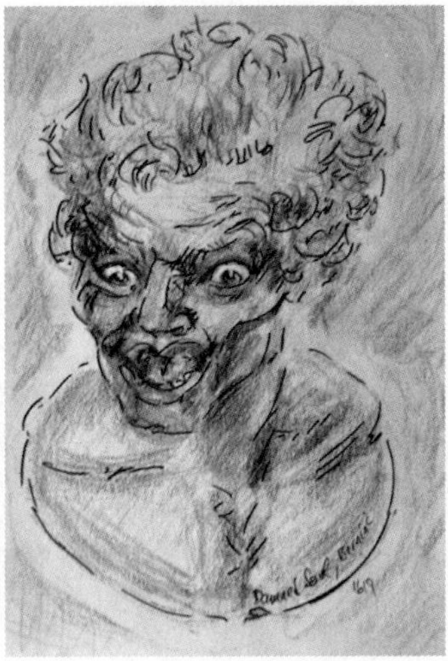

We went through your HELL!

All the way back
Church zealots
Convinced our own ancestry,
T'seduweh,
Of their HELL-bound ways.

We innocent children lost
Our own faith
In humanity

Even hope
Became
That beam of sunlight

Shining, yes,
But always somewhere else.

## Ghosts

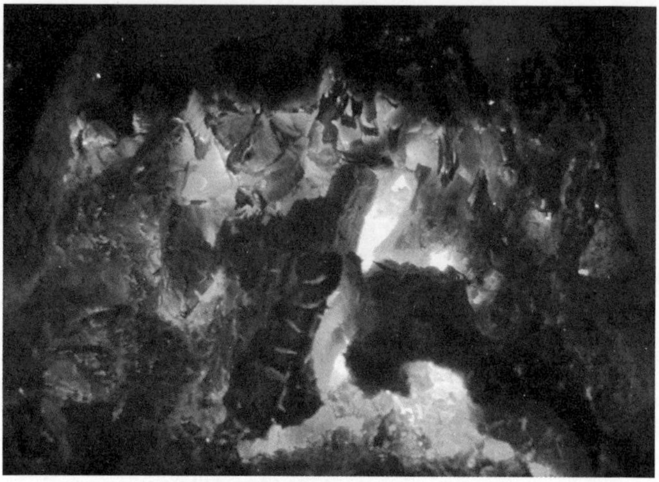

Flames
In both, zealotry
and Indigenous

One, a dire warning
Of eternal damnation

The other, Our Relatives
Come to keep us company
With flashed fortunes

One has lost its Power,
Its stigmatic grip, wounds that just won't heal.
Ours, with Ceremonial Water,

Not meant to take apart and destroy.
This Healing,
Brings Back LIFE Eternal

## The Looong Sleep

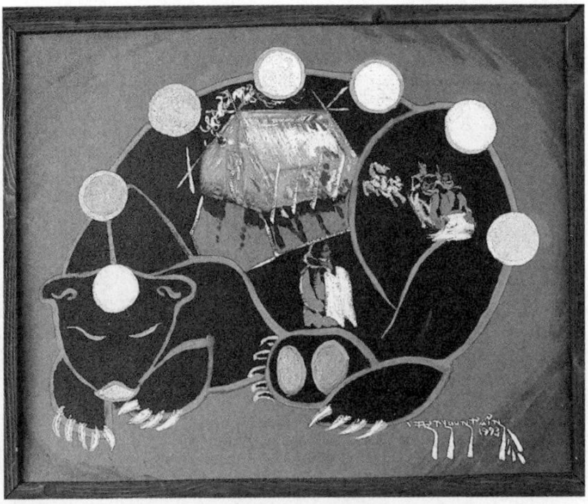

Like Sah, Bear,
We had the Looong Sleep,
Only vague dreams of a distant Home.

First a number, Mine 249
And smell of coal oil,
Over shaven heads.

We prayed by rote,
In strange Latin litany
Sleep-Walking through Dark months
Of this soul-chilling numb.

Many never woke back up,
Just stole the rest
Of the Looong Night.

Most, just plain Angry,
Lashing out at any touch,
Any Love.

## Seh K'eh T'ieh, Charcoal on Wood

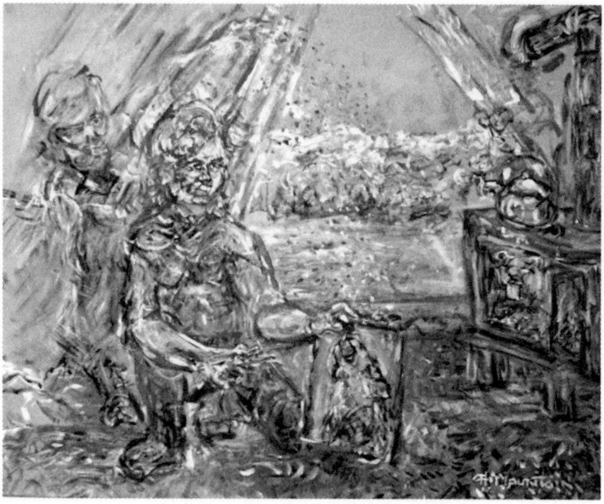

THiS I Always Knew,
Of Myself, an ARTIST

Able to shape out
From early morning
Pinkish sunlight
Through shifting shades

Of morning Mountain blues

Images of Wolf,
Bear and Eagle

To smoothed, chopped firewood
My first of Art.

Only to see it
ALL go to family heat
And camping comfort.

**We Didn't Have It Easy**

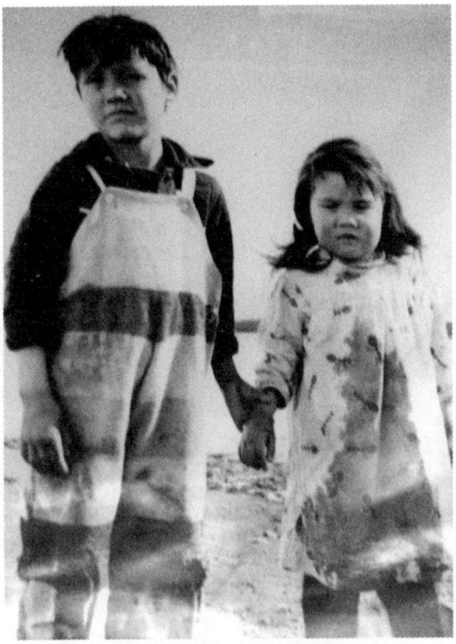

Some, like sis Judy,
Were more or less tomboys.

She always wanted to
Follow brother
Play with the boys.

We played Rough!

Most times I'd have to bring her back
Like This,
Big red ants on her dress,
Covered in mud!

But that was US.

A Free Life,
But not easy.

## A Friend for Life

We met them from all over—

Having come in late to the Grollier Hall Residential School in late September of 1959. I snuck into Grade 3.

No one said anything as I picked a seat way in the back.

The nun, Sister Leduc, made it a point to hand out paper money for correct answers. By Christmas I was sitting right in the front, a big pile of paper bills in front of me. For a final $5 she asked to have the word "wasps" spelled. I did.

Sister Leduc said that since I had the most money, I could have first pick from a row of toys on a shelf above the classroom. I asked her what happens to the ones with no money, and could I give my pick to someone else.

"It's your choice, Antoine, what you want to do," says she.

I chose Roy Goose, an Inuvaluit from the remote Ulukhaktok, even further north from where we were in the High Arctic. Li'l Roy was always busy drawing jets. I was impressed the li'l guy actually invented stuff, like the transistor radio he played 'til late at night, the CBC station, CHAK's Late Show, Floyd Cramer's "Last Date" featured.

Roy was so proud when he heard his name being called. They put a chair on top of a desk and he reached for a big red firetruck. I had made a friend for life.

He later joined the Air Force, was a successful CBC radio announcer, was an expert in his language and native culture, and an outstanding photographer besides.

The lower of these photos he took for a *Macleans* story on residential schools. The fireweed is our sign for hope, the first to return after a wildfire.

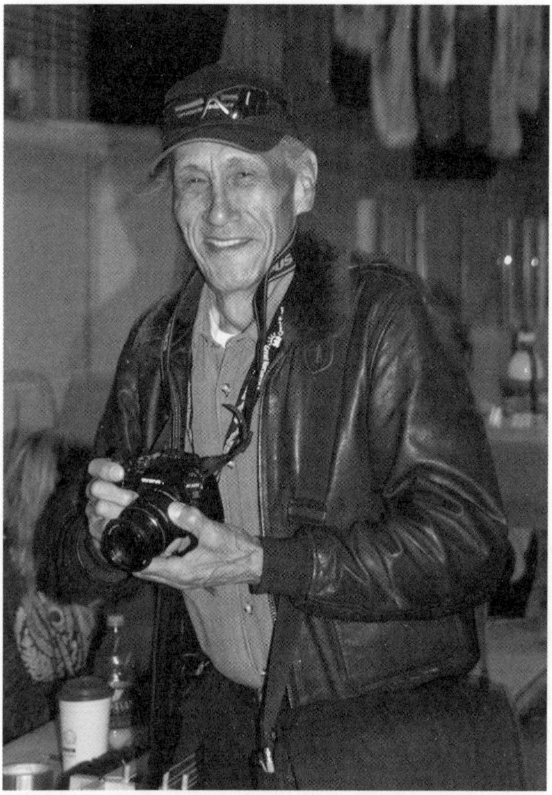

Roy Goose, a friend for life.

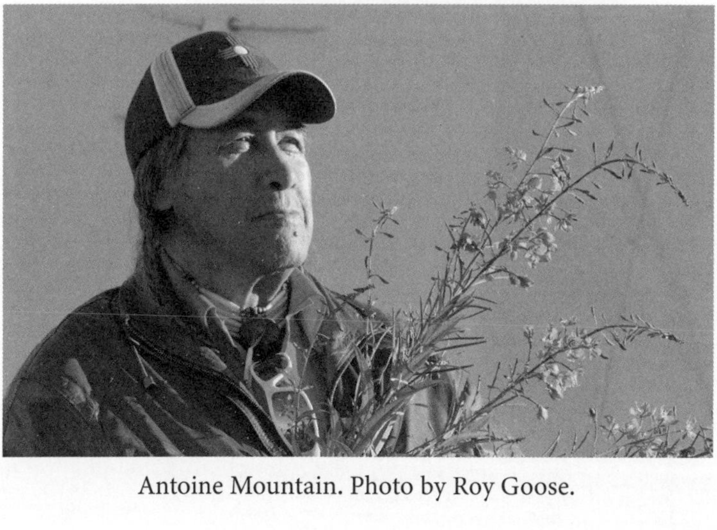

Antoine Mountain. Photo by Roy Goose.

## What I Had in Mind

That Study in POWER!

THIS. Italian Sculptor Bernini's and the Divine Michelangelo's DAVID, is what I had in mind all along.

For obvious reasons we were never on the same page as our captors: the priests and nuns. Even our teachers at the school were pretty well conscripted to drop whatever comforts they had in the South to work in the world's coldest little place Inuvik.

The government town was specifically built with assimilation in mind, turning little brown Indians and Inuit into your typical Whites.

The priests and nuns, as their secretive selves, found out who was good at what and got you to do it for them.

I found myself up on a ladder, with a projected image for me to copy in paint on the upper wall. Earlier artists did strictly religious paintings, the renderer as familiar with desert peasants as the Man on the Moon.

I only wanted to use my own colours, to bring the drab scene to some kinda life, a major no-no.

Being of a naturally rebellious kind, I got down off the ladder to success and let them know to find someone else. Back to thirty below freezing with the rest outside!

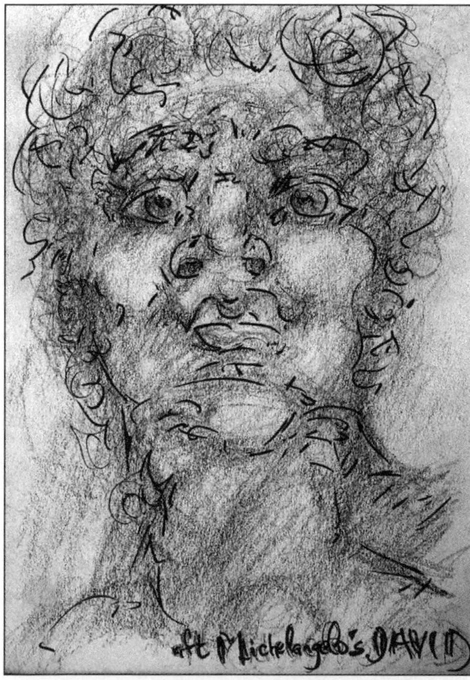
aft Michelangelo's DAVID

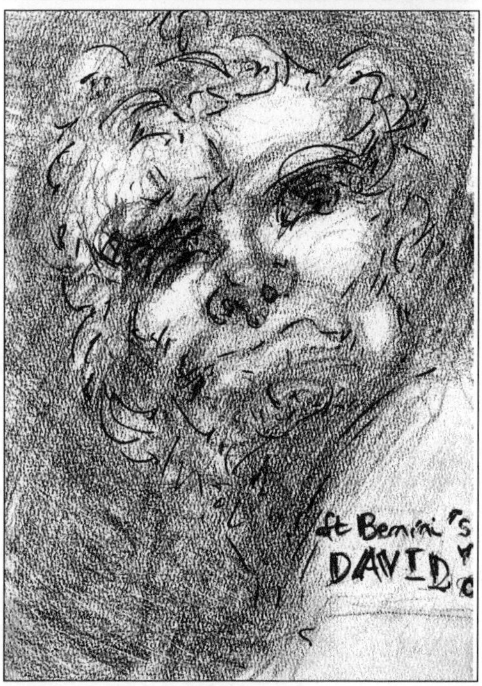
aft Bernini's
DAVID

## Grollier, A Fort Knox of PAIN!

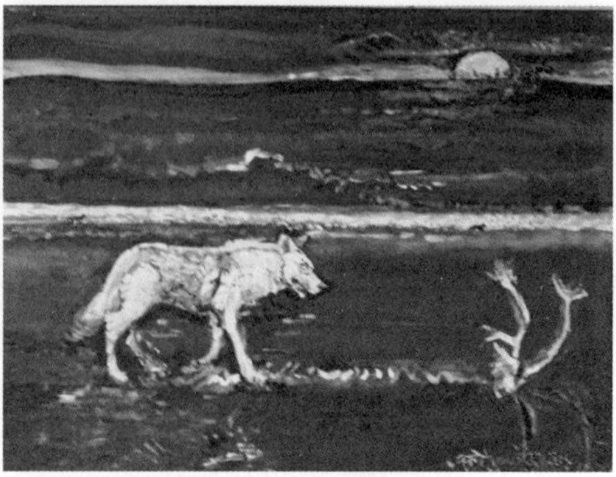

Grollier Hall, in Inuvik, eventually became one of the most notorious of sexual abuse schools brought before the courts of law. The place stank of religious front to an abyss of human torture. You had to pretty well watch your every move, especially with the 'Sister's Pets', snitching on you so you'd miss the weekly movie or get a strapped for uttering a Dene or Inuit word.

When the offer came up to try cross-country ski racing me and my best friend, John T'Seleie grabbed at the chance. The first sets of skis we got were old Army issue. Our poles, broken hockey sticks.

This tells you how badly we wanted to just get out of the Prison to Shame. We had lit tracks across a broad field, back and forth, every super-chilly evening. Doing well was another mountain to climb.

Like Beleh, wolves, we just kept a steady pace, waiting for the real race to start.

## Fiehkan K'eh

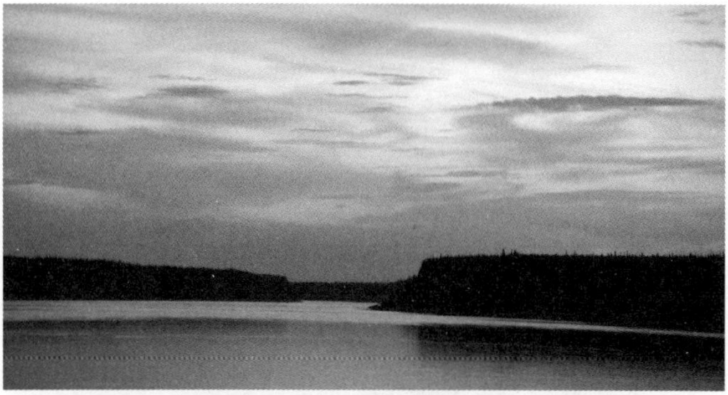

It stays, in the mind's eye.

All winter,
Far, far away
We dreamed of
The majestic Ramparts
Cliffs fall straight down
200 feet, to the Duhogah
Big River

and close to the end
Of our stay
In the dread Grollier Hall
We talked of nothing else,
But Fiddlesticks,
Our swimming hole

Or just sitting on these shores
'Hooking', Fishing
The Sa Ra-ahyileh, Midnight Sun away!

## My Little Heart of ICE!

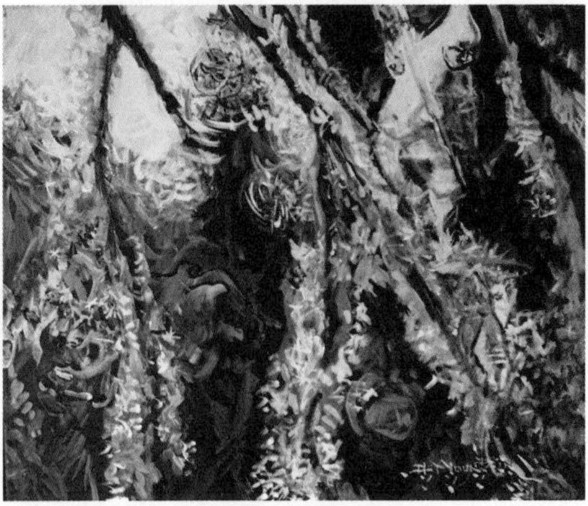

.. at only 12
After three years
.. of this Hell
I could feel
The warmth of Human
Leave the Dene me, with every breath.
For yet three more
My Spring
Would not come back
...

I could see
Other frozen smiles
All around.

**Rayuka**

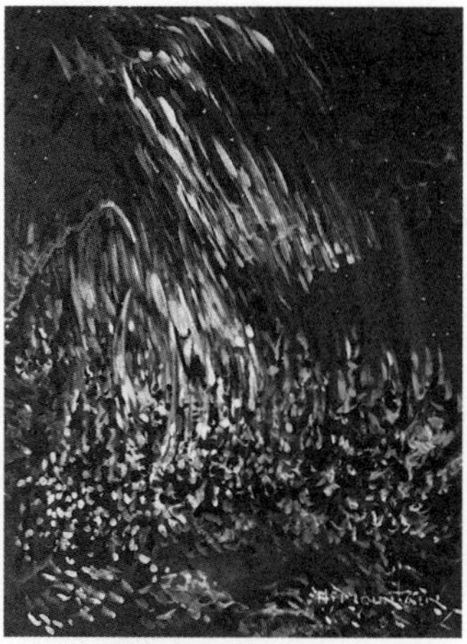

To the Dene
These dancing, restless
Spirits,

Northern Lights,
Not quite Here on Earth
And neither where all else go
After life... and Before?
Even amongst us, too close to touch,
Suicides, deaths, far too many.

And now the thousands,
Missing and murdered

From our Circles

Some memories

Come with Warnings

Rayuka!

## The Old Style, It's an Art

Whilst away at these confining residential schools, this is what we were Missing out on.

For gah, rabbits, you find their little trails, usually marked by li'l round turds.

Find a spot with a sturdy enough tree beside the tracks and set up with a crossbar and block in the rest of the trap, with little sticks and pieces of willow, so there's only one opening in the middle.

Cut a long pole, heavy enough on one end to lift the caught rabbit. Balance the heavy end on a branch and swing it down to the snare spot.

Tie your long snare-string to the smaller end, bring it down, and loop it around a short trip-stick on the string, a couple of inches long. Run the string to the other end of your li'l trip-stick, loop to hanging, and make a loop big enough for the rabbit head, hanging close to the ground. Place thin brace-sticks on each side of the loop to keep it open.

Set up like that, your gah, rabbit, will hang several feet off the ground, safe from any martens, foxes, or even tah soh, raven.

There is always the magic moment.

You pop your hands off the set-up... hold your breath. When it holds, your gah, rabbit snare is ready!

These olde-styles were meant to give you what you want without any kind of less damage.

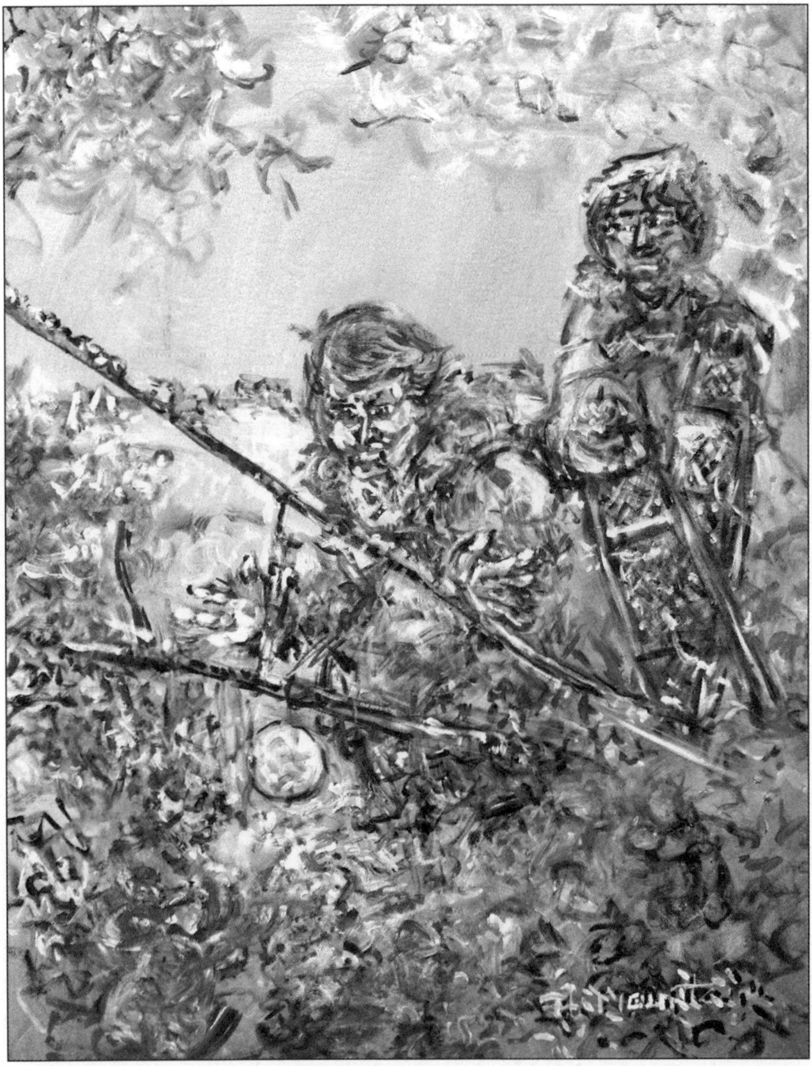

## Sa Ra-ahyileh

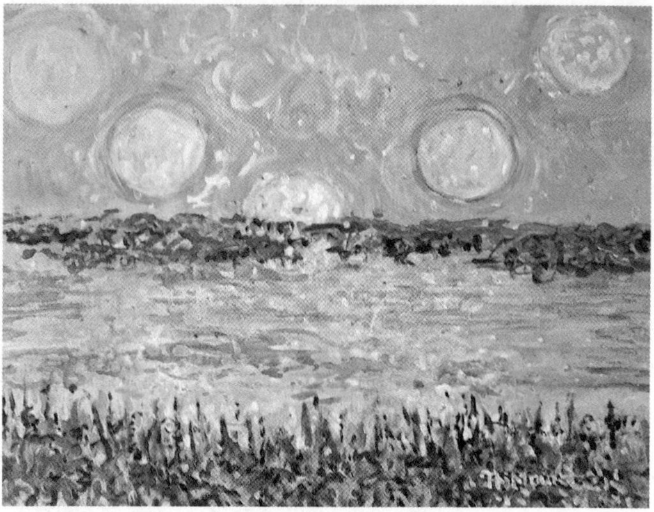

We never knew each other.

Just little strangers
Fighting to make it

Past ten long months

Away

From Sa hRa-ahyeieh, Midnight Sun

Dreaming of sparkling waters
To jump into
A bottomless Heaven

Our Homeland playground

In Eternal SUN!

## Shih K'e Koh, Fire on the Mountain

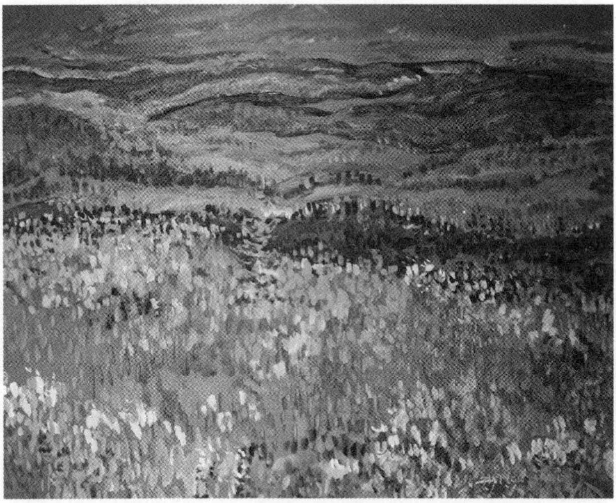

In a World Apart
We ARE

Like the Fireweed,
First to Come Back

After Wildfires,

Like the Whiteman's Church
In Our World Apart
We Thrive ON

Untouched

As EVER

## 'Til Tomorrow

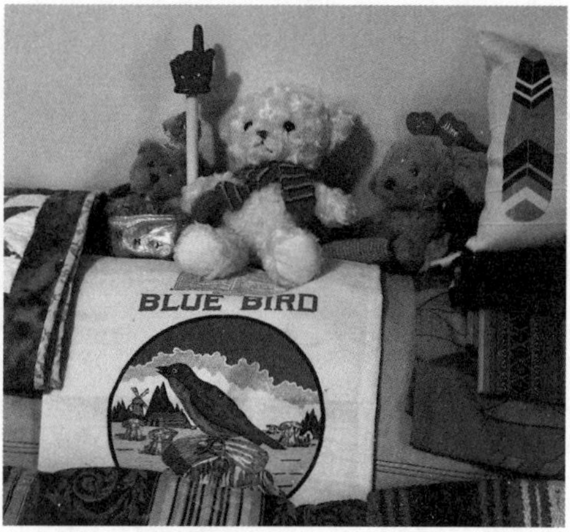


Yes, you've lost That part,
Your precious Childhood.

Imagine a Playground,
With just the shadows of running feet.

Empty pauses to laughter
We Were there, a lifetime of energy
... On Pause ...
Not even of
The Present. Just over there,
Someplace.

Yet Some don't
Ever go away.
Your little team-mates, the 249'ers!
MY #! ... Cheering you ON
'Til Tomorrow.

## Brothers-in-Arms, of Truth

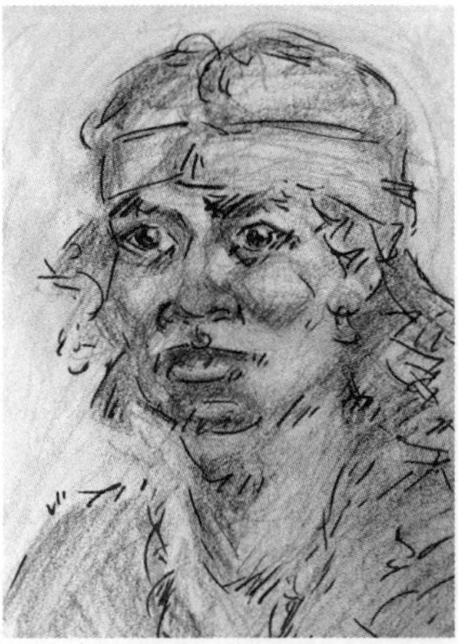

One thing we have in common with our southern Dineh, Navajo relatives is our residential schools, their boarding schools. Both sought a cultural genocide, for us to lose our very Indigenous identity, languages, and cultural ways.

Early on, in early 1990, I made it a point to begin visiting on the Big Navajo Reservation in Arizona and New Mexico. Now, almost forty years later I know for sure I made the right choice.

Members of the Navajo Nation were enlisted into the American Army, as Code Talkers. They used the language they were forbidden to speak to save democracy itself.

In Canada we now face a similar annihilation of our Peoples. With the Missing and Murdered Children's unmarked graves found in Kamloops, BC and across the country, we now dealing with genocide. No less. Humanity itself is being held hostage by the missing and real history of western civilization.

## Nuthin' Left to Give

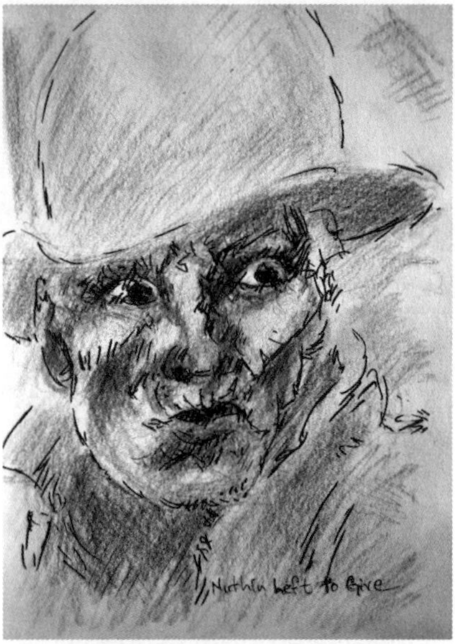


THIS is the feeling
You were left with
Even long after leaving
Residential school
So used to following orders
With severe punishment if not.
We didn't know normal
You had to be reminded
You have a mind of your own
Even FREE!
... and at last
Dene again.

## In Every Tree

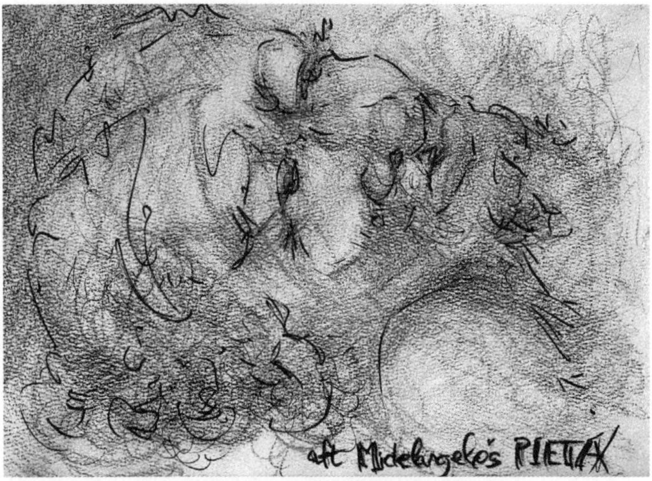


His words, His teachings
Were nothing new

To the Dene,
Our faith
Hope and charity
We already lived

A sharing culture needs not
Say 'ours is
The Only Way'

What is sad,
He lived in vain,

His Truths

Hung,
Unpicked fruit,
In every tree.

## The Last Leaf

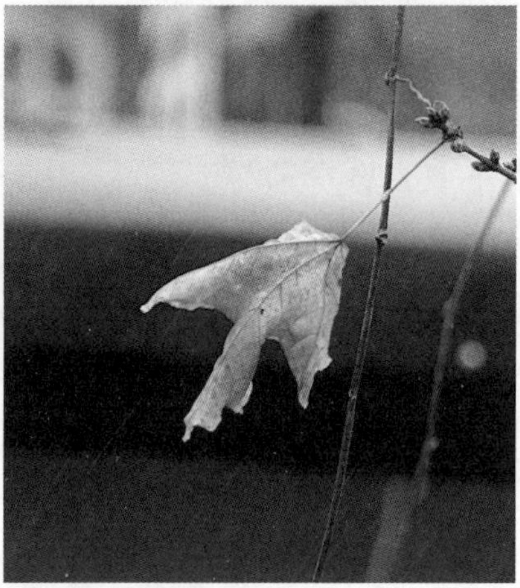

.. It remains! ...

Whenever I see this,
After another hard, freezing winter

Just that one battered leaf,
A tattered flag, after its battles,
Just hanging in the winds ...

I get to thinking
Of all of us

Hundreds of little lost souls,
Through a cultural, genocidal
Grind

We've survived, yes
But in a strange
Twist of fate,
Hold the country together.

## Rakeh Noh

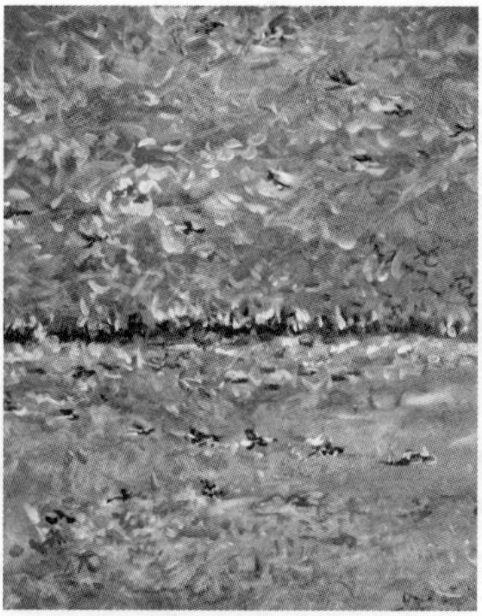

... It remains! ...
... Not much had changed ...

In the end,
After all the years
Of Pain

Many simply shut down,
Emotions in limbo
To a timeless trauma.

Yet the land was always the same,
Just a little out of reach.

We missed the times we needed
To be fully Dene.

Yet not quite even human

The land, Rakeh Noh, Our Mother,
Like the geese,
Takes us back.

**Koh Ak'oneh Yieh!**

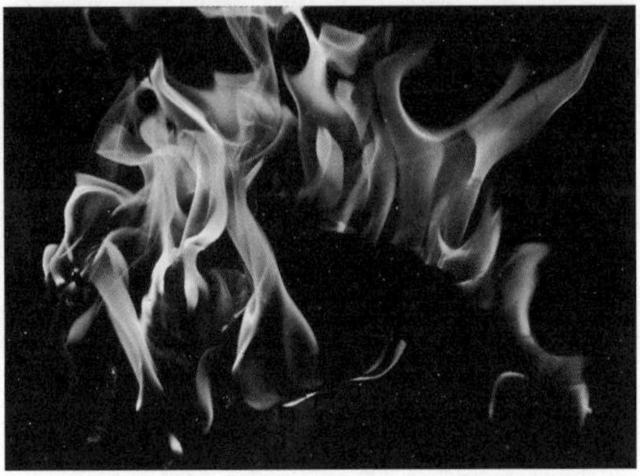

All across our lonely evening skies

A Sacred Voice is calling
The names of the ten thousand

Or More

The Little, the Missing
And Murdered
CHILDREN

Marked only
By every Dat'sedebih Ahdzieh,
Wishing MooN,
Mother MooN

To Her promised awakening

Of an eternal Dawn

In a New FIRE!

## Our Dene Heaven

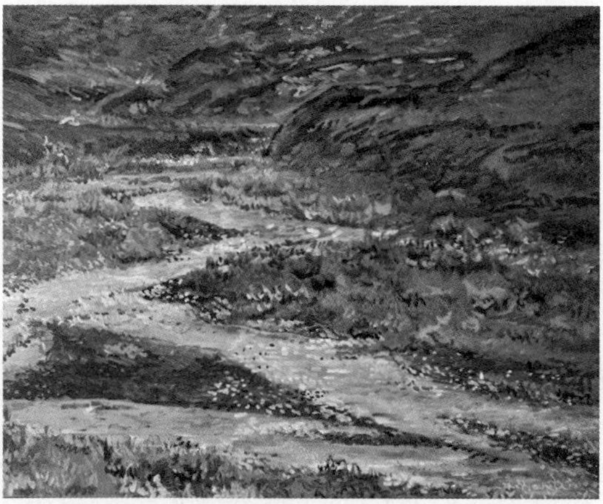

... to Ceremony...

As I sit to vigil,
Recalling them endless nights
Of muffled tears

A Vision
Comes

A high-country mountain stream,
The only sound,

Soft melodies,
Winds over ripples

Of this Peace
I won't ever awaken from

Our Dene Heaven!

**A Second LIFE**

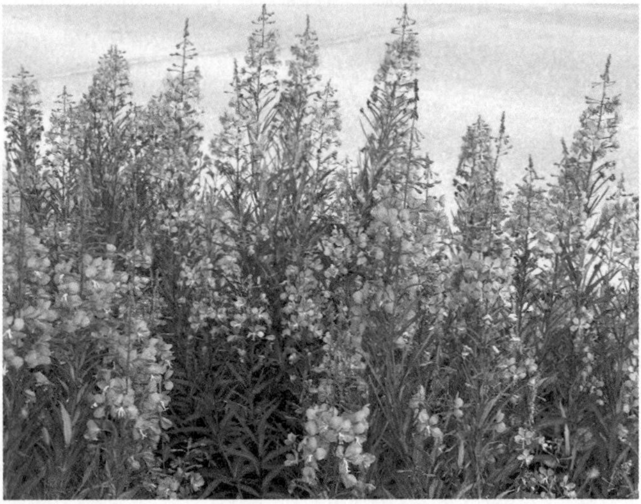

Another chance ...

Lightning strikes
Out of the blue yonder

Wildfires
Leave smoking, charred remains

To somehow survive.
Out of the same blue
Fireweed, HOPE
Even out of gravel

The first to return
To rebuild
Our Future

## Our Wishing Wells

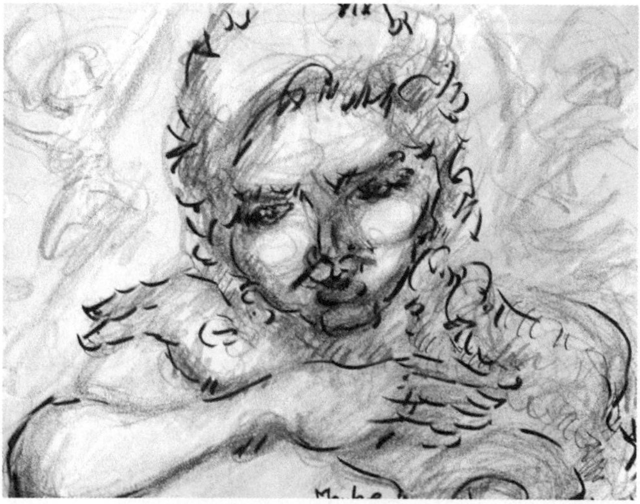

... of hopes ... in dreams

Eyes closed, we toss our fate
Into the deep
Man-made chasms, our scattered muses.

... a wayward history

Deep below, floating
On Life, rising

Our drum
To language in song

.. and just at twilight
Through distant rainbows

Misted female rains

Come for us.

## Child of LIGHT!

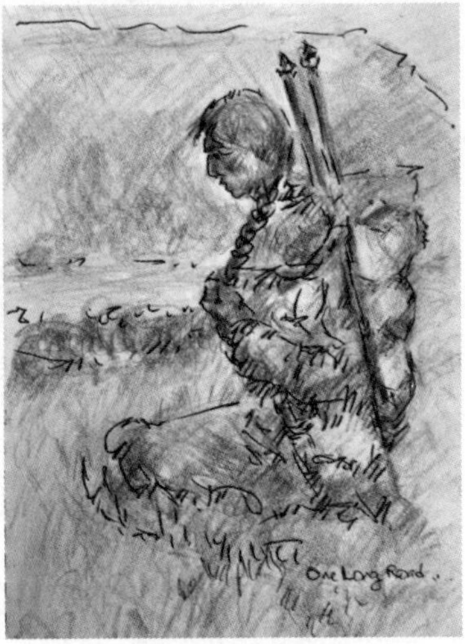

As does Summer run into arms of
Brilliant Fall.
So do we, Children of LIGHT!

Run back to the arms of Mother,
Out of hidden shadows,
Let her sooth this stumble,
From the Circle.

Flickering leaves of birch,
First to turn the brightest. Sun Yellow!

Play along a long lost
Drum Song. From yon stream.

And Your Child within,
Held in

WOLF Spirit!

## Ghost Birds

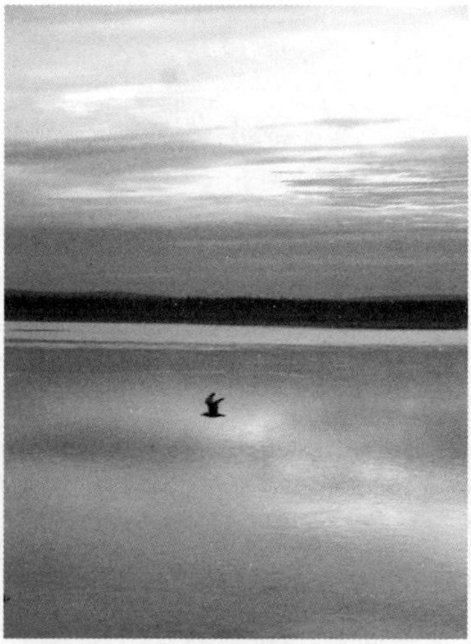

A flight
Out of enjewelled blue,
Far above

These passing days

In each a memory
To dust by now
In all but Life.

There are the trails
We yet must weave

Into the Light's golden band
Belted, Missing

Each dream

Still in Wing.

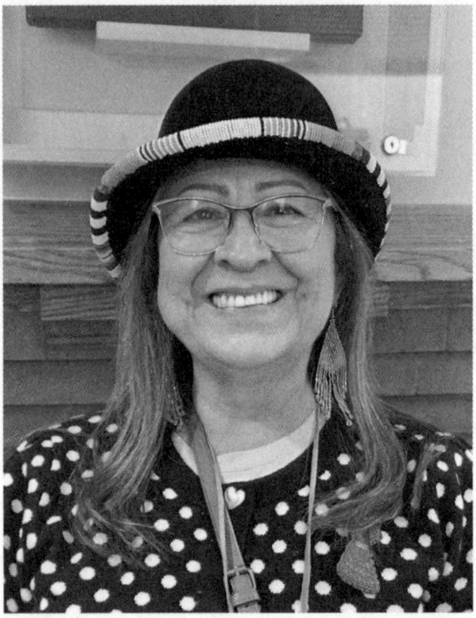

## DORENE BERNARD

Kesatum tan teli L'nuwey, Kiwnik Clan, Sipekne'katik, Mi'kmaki, is a traditional Mi'kmaq woman, of the Sipekne'katik Band, residing in Indian Brook, Nova Scotia. She is a Survivor of the Shubenacadie Indian Residential School, the third generation to attend within her family. She works with Survivors and families in the Atlantic region to document the history of the IRS Legacy and Survivors' profiles for the archives, and IRS Commemorations and is a member of the Elders Advisory Council at Mi'kmawey Debert Cultural Centre.

## Water Teachings

by Dorene Bernard

Teluisi, Kesatum tan teli L'nui,
Kiwnik uk'totem, Telawi,
Sipekne'katik, aq Mi'kmak'i.
Grassroots Grandmother, Water Walker,
Water Protector, Treaty Defender, Survivor

I AM HUMBLED to be asked to share Water Teachings in this book and ask that you take what is helpful for your understanding. You will have many Elders' Teachings during your lifetime, as I have, and there will be those that you embrace, practice, and share with others.

I love and acknowledge the many Indigenous Knowledge Keepers, Elders, Ceremony Leaders, Grandmothers and Grandfathers, Sukwis and Nklamuksis, many of whom are now my Ancestors, who have guided me with love and patience and gifted me their teachings over the past 35 years.

As a survivor of the Shubenacadie Indian Residential School, I spent the first half of my life just trying to survive the trauma I went through there, and after I left there. I spent my youth and young adult years searching for and finding my identity, culture, and purpose in life. This past half of my life has been learning to heal, and walking my path, and doing the work of heart and spirit.

I want to share some of these teachings with you about the sacredness of Water, Samqwan, as you learn about Netukulimk and the impacts on Water, Mother Earth, and climate justice. These teachings also speak to the social, cultural, and spiritual aspects of your life, and how you can put them into action through what you say, what you do, and how you think about your connection to the Water.

**Sacred Water**

The life, culture, and strength of Indigenous Peoples cannot be separated from the sacredness of Water. The Earth is our Mother and provides all that is needed to live. The Water is her life blood, and we must all remember that Water is precious, Water is alive, it has spirit, Water is life. Today, many have forgotten their sacred relationship with the Water and Mother Earth.

Water is always central in Indigenous cultural practices and ceremonies. Water holds great significance in the teachings and ceremonies of sweat lodge, fasting, Sundance, rites of passage, in prayers, and medicines of healing, in songs, all that helped me to heal, gain good health and understanding, over the past 35 years. Many sacred ceremonies connect us to the land and Water and Ancestors in profound ways. During the fast ceremony, we go without food and Water for four day/nights, alone, on the land, in prayer and sacrifice for those who are

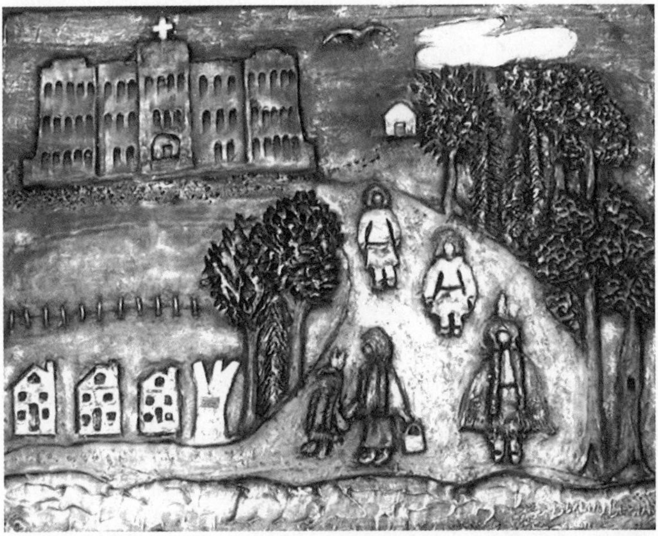

Dorene's clay tile painting that represents "Freedom Road" that shows her family walking away from residential school.

sick, for our Mother Earth and Water, for the good of all our Relations. During this time, you develop a sacred relationship with the Water. Your love, gratitude, and respect for the Water become intense as you pray, deepen your understanding, and embrace the teaching that Water is life.

Indigenous Peoples embrace that life emanates from Water and we must have access to the land and clean Water to survive. We are all Survivors, as we carry the ancestral memory in our DNA of historic trauma of colonization, systemic racism, oppression, residential school, infringement on Human Rights and Indigenous Rights, and the impacts on our families and communities, our lands and Waters. Our L'nu ways of Netukulimk, guidance of our Creator, our Ancestors and Indigenous Knowledge Keepers,

Grandmothers, have helped us to heal and gain understanding, resilience, and strength to survive. This is what the rest of the world needs to learn, so that all life, our Nokomaq, can all survive in these times of climate crises.

The Women's Teachings portray the role of women as sacred beings, life-givers — gifted with the ability to bring new life into this world. Women carry the child in the womb; surrounded and protected by Water. We drink the Water, breathe the Water, and we are over 70 percent Water. When we are born, we come through the Water, carrying the spirit of the Water when we take our first breath of air in this world.

Women have also been given the responsibility to protect the Water on Mother Earth, not only for their child, but for all life. This includes all that cannot speak, all our Nokomaq, the land, the animals, flyers, swimmers, crawlers, plants and trees and rocks, and the future generations that need clean Water to live.

Women carry many rituals and ceremonies that include the Water: birth ceremony, death ceremony, grief and loss ceremony, moon ceremony, healing and Water ceremonies, and more. Water is central to Women's roles in teaching that we are a part of Creation, Msit Nokomaq, interconnected and interdependent. It is our responsibility to practice these teachings while caring for our families and communities: growing, preparing and cooking foods, nurturing and washing our babies, and protecting the health of the Water and our environment, which contributes to the health of our families and communities.

Women's role as Protectors of the land and the Water, is to teach and uphold these spiritual teachings. In asserting our inherent rights and responsibilities we must uphold the L'nu laws of Netukulimk, taking only what is necessary to sustain life and protecting the integrity of Mother Earth and Water to leave what is needed for all future generations. Elder Dr. Albert Marshall, Sr. has said,

> Netukulimk is the use of the natural bounty provided by the Creator for the self-support and well-being of the individual and the community. Netukulimk is achieving adequate standards of community nutrition and economic well-being.

As a traditional grandmother, I learned about the Mother Earth Water Walk and Grandmother Josephine Mandamin-ba, who began this Water Ceremony in 2003, walking around the Great Lakes. In 2007, I began to hold Water ceremony here in Mi'kmaki to amplify her voice and what Grandmother Josephine and the Water Walkers were doing to raise awareness of the pollution of the Water on Mother Earth. We walked for the Water with Grandmother Josephine and other Water Walkers and Mi'kmak'i grandmothers who came together for wise counsel and teachings where the Women shared the Water teachings, drumming, singing, and education.

Mi'kmak'i Grassroots Grandmothers worked to build an alliance with others who wanted to work together in reconciliation, with respect, reciprocity, and responsibility to protect the Water and the Land. Many environmental issues with impacts to the Water were discussed by those who joined us from across Mi'kmak'l. Our purpose was to take action on Alton Gas storage, fracking waste, ocean turbines, gold mining, quarry expansion, and the lack of fish passage in the Bay of Fundy. We also wanted to stand against the many other threats to the Water that keep coming as governments and corporations continue planning oil and gas extraction, aggregate and rare earth mining, gold mining, and uranium projects. All of these things will impact the clean Water, Air, and Lands that all life needs to survive.

We didn't know it then, but we were being prepared to stand together to protect our Water here in Sipekne'katik, Mi'kmaki, on the Shubenacadie River, when we learned about the Alton Gas/AltaGas project in 2007. Grassroots Grandmothers were doing Water ceremony for the river before Alton Gas came to our territory. It has taken years of frontline resistance, beginning with prayer and Pipe ceremony, with the Grassroots People, Water Protectors, Land defenders, Warriors, and those who sacrificed their time and bodies on the front line, away from their children, families and communities.

My Sipekne'katik Band was in litigation in the Nova Scotia Supreme Court against Alton Gas and the Province of Nova Scotia for several years, and our Mi'kmaq women were arrested while protecting the Water. There was a campaign of continuous public education on Environmental Racism, Ceremonial Water Walks, Indigenous science knowledge, and ally solidarity. Actions were taken in the boardrooms, on the screen in the documentary *There's Something in the Water* and all those Water Protectors and allies who were behind the scenes, organizing and fundraising at rallies, and marches.

Indigenous Elders and Omen were speaking at universities and public places to inform the public about the environmental laws being broken and the infringement on Mi'kmaq Treaty Rights. We finally stopped Alton Gas from desecrating our Shubenacadie River Watershed. Their plans were to extract the Water, replace it with salt brine mining waste, and contribute to climate change by building 18 salt caverns over a proposed 50-year project. This work would not have been possible without our People's sacrifice and commitment to the protection of the land and Water. We couldn't have done this without the guidance and protection of our Ancestors and Creator. I always keep everyone in my prayers of thanksgiving.

Water is sacred and we need to protect it for all life that depends on clean Water to live.

**Water Protection**

The Alton Gas Resistance brought together grassroots Grandmothers from Mi'kmaki, the Native Women's Association, environmental organizations, and many allies to protect Water and uphold Mi'kmaq Treaty Rights. We welcomed the December 2021 announcement that Alton Gas was decommissioning its project. The Province of Nova Scotia and the proponent never consulted with Sipekne'katik or respected our consultation process. Although ordered by the courts to consult with Mi'kmaq leaders, they chose instead to decommission the project. We hoped this would include removing pipelines, restoring wetlands, and repairing damage to the land and Water along the riverside. We also wanted assurance that the infrastructure could not later be sold for fracking or waste disposal in our river.

Sipekne'katik, Mi'kmaq Water Protectors, Treaty Rights holders, and allies sought the return of these lands for stewardship as compensation for the infringement of our Treaty Rights and Title, and for seven years of sacrifice and anguish. Water Protectors lived at the Treaty camp, conducted research, and filed Freedom of Information requests to obtain documents showing that Nova Scotia Environment, the Department of Fisheries and Oceans, and the Province were breaking their own laws.

Three Mi'kmaq women Water Protectors were charged for standing on the front line and holding the proponent, the Nova Scotia Government, and the Environment Department accountable for their lack of meaningful consultation and disregard for Mi'kmaq Treaty Rights. L'nu laws and Netukulimk guide our responsibilities and our spiritual and cultural connection to this river. The women were later restricted from the site, but the charges were eventually dismissed.

In 2007, consultation between the Government, Alton Gas, and Sipekne'katik, combined with transparency, strong environmental laws, and protection for the river and species at risk, should have been enough to safeguard the Shubenacadie River and all life within its watershed. This process failed, and all Nova Scotians should be concerned. Governments must be held accountable for protecting Water, land, and all species, while upholding Mi'kmaq Treaty Rights and our free, prior, and informed consent.

**Protectors and Defenders**

Across Turtle Island, Indigenous Water Protectors and land defenders are on the front lines of extractive industry and development, to protect the Water. Extractive corporations and land developers are permitted to run roughshod over the people, lands, and waters by governments that are corrupted by power and greed.

There are Indigenous communities that still do not have access to clean drinking water in Canada in 2026. Chronic health issues impact communities due to the lack of clean water, quality water infrastructure, poor maintenance and lack of political will to build water facilities that most Canadian take for granted. Communities are still being poisoned by the pollution of their Water.

Environmental racism in Canada impacts Indigenous, Black, and poor communities that are impacted by industry and the pollution of their water and lands, and their bodies, resulting in chronic illnesses and death of those who live in their shadows.

There is a direct correlation to violence against Indigenous Women around the world; and the many Missing and Murdered Indigenous Women and Girls and relatives, in communities nearby. Many women have been murdered and have gone missing while standing on the front lines against the oil and gas extraction industries, at the hands of corporate security, governments, state police and military. Many more men and boys have also been murdered or have gone missing, while defending the women and children in their remote communities.

We have witnessed what happened to the Wet'suet'en and Gidimt'en, Lakota, Dakota, Nakota, and Anishnabek, Wolastoqiyik, Mi'kmaq, and other Indigenous and allies across Turtle Island who have taken a stand to protect their unceded lands and resources from oil and gas pipelines and extractive industries. Reporters and those who have documented the many human rights atrocities of the state

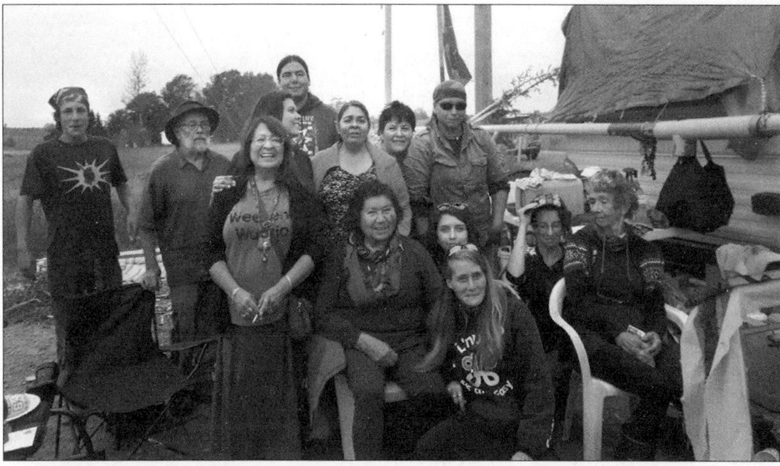

A few Mi'kmaq and Allies Water Protectors at Stop Alton Gas
Felix Pulnaq, Martial Thiebaux, Dorene Bernard, Eliza Knockwood, Dale Poulette, Carol Ducie Howe, Sandra Sack, Paul Isaac, Grandmother Josephine Mandamin, Jade Knockwood, Nika Peters, Annabelle Mott, Stewart Thibeaux, and Marian Nicholas.

have been arrested and charged for sharing the truth to the world. This is happening across the globe, where people stand on the front lines to stop oil and gas extraction, stop climate change, and protect Mother Earth and the Water. The land and Water have been bought and sold, destroyed by industry and governments that only see them as commodities. The lands and Water and people, animals and all life that are destroyed are viewed as collateral damage and inconvenience, expendable to their quest for wealth and greed.

Indigenous Peoples and allies are being criminalized for standing up to protect their Water and lands for their families, Nations and the life of future generations. Governments and police have over-reaching powers that can be used to protect the pipelines against the Indigenous protection of our lands and Waters and imprison those who stand up to stop the continued destruction and causes of global climate change.

We are at a crossroads where every human being is called to stand in solidarity with Peoples across Mother Earth. We must stand together wherever Water and lands are at risk from industrial desecration, environmental racism, fossil fuel infrastructure, climate change, and the state laws, violence, and greed that have put lives at risk in the past and continue to do so today. These threats also endanger the lives of future generations.

Knowledge Keepers have been sharing the teachings and prophecies about what is happening on Mother Earth for years. One of these prophecies says there will come a time when an ounce of Water will be more valuable than an ounce of gold. No matter how much money or gold you have, you will not be able to buy that Water because of how precious it is. You can't drink gold. Another prophecy I learned says that the next World War will not be fought over oil and gas, but over clean Water.

We call on everyone to stand up and take responsibility and action for what is right and just, for the protection of the land and water, that we all need to survive. The climate crises are caused by the actions or inactions of humankind. Only we can do something to change it.

With the continuing political capture by extractive corporations, mining, and oil and gas, and development, our lands and Waters and all species that live in Mi'kmaki are under continuous threat of exploitation, pollution, destruction, and climate change. We rely on our science and environmental stewardship and unity of all people to protect the sacred for all future generations, all life that do not have a voice, all our Nokomaq.

**Honour Your Water**

There are some things you can do, wherever you are:

- Embrace your relationship with the Water; Tell the Water you love, thank and respect the Water, every day.
- Speak for the Water, even when your voice shakes, and you don't feel you are being heard. Kisu'lk hears you. The Water hears you and our Ancestors hear you.
- Embrace the laws of Netukulimk to protect the land and Water for all life to survive now and for our future generations, and hold governments accountable to uphold these natural laws.
- Participate in Water Walks, Water ceremonies and support education to learn about impacts to the Water and learn where your Water comes from. We pray for the Water and our unceded

lands that have sustained Mi'kmaki for over thirteen-thousand years, and raise awareness of the sacredness of Water and our relationship with our Nokomaq.

- Remember those who do not have access to clean drinking water and find ways to support them, advocate, participate in actions to end boil water advisories and Do Not Consume orders in their communities and have free access to clean water. Find out what you can do to help their fight for justice, to get remedy for decades of pollution, poisoning their water. They need health care and healing and to know they are not forgotten.
- Honour your Water, protect the Water, pray for the Water, sing for the Water.
- Remember the People and Water and Lands across Mi'kmaki that have been impacted by industry and development that contaminated their Waters: Pictou Landing First Nation, Shelburne, Harrietsfield, Lincolnville, Sydney, Dartmouth Lakes Charles, Thomas, and other locations.

**Solidarity and Actions**

Remember the successful solidarity and actions of Mi'kmaq and Allies that were taken in Mi'kmaki that helped to stop industrial desecration and climate change before they could destroy our lands and Waters:

- Elsipogtog stopped SWN from fracking in their territory.

- Unamaki stopped Petroworth from fracking at Lake Ainsle.
- Sipekne'katik stopped Alton Gas/Altagas from destroying the Shubie River and lands.
- Mi'kmaki stopped LNG terminal and mancamps – but they are back now, with Chiefs in Nova Scotia giving their consent. Sipekne'katik and Millbrook have not consented to this project or mancamps!
- Save Owls Head Provincial Park stopped the Nova Scotia government and Wealthy foreigners from selling our unceded Mi'kmaki and protecting the land/Water.
- Hunter's Mountain, Unamaki, Mi'kmaki protected the forests, the animals, and the Water that have sustained our communities.

We can take action to protect the Water when we learn of development that fails to protect the Water, the life that depends on it, and future generations. When we stand for the Water and the land, we stand for all people, as well as the animals, flyers, swimmers, crawlers, burrowers, insects, plants, trees, and all living beings that rely on clean Water to survive. We must think carefully about what we want to leave behind for the next seven generations living on Mother Earth.

Wela'liek.

# Water Carrier

by Dorene Bernard

Nin teluisi, Kesatum tan teli Lnu'wey.
Kiwnik uk'totem, Sipekne'katik Tele'awi, Mi'kmaki'k.

**Personal Journey**

In 2007, I learned about the Mother Earth Water Walk and Grandmother Josephine Mandamin, who was leading the Lake Erie Water Walk and was in her fifth year of walking and praying for the Waters of the Great Lakes. Her story deeply resonated with me. I began following her journey online and felt called to do something here in Mi'kmaki to help amplify the voices of the Water Walkers and raise awareness about water pollution and the urgent need to protect the Waters that all life on Mother Earth depends upon.

That same year, during a Shake Tent ceremony, I received guidance through prayer that inspired me to start the Grassroots Grandmothers Circle. I began meeting with people in my community and with representatives from other First Nations across Wabanaki and the Atlantic region to discuss the issues affecting our communities, including social justice, environmental concerns, and Treaty Rights. We also invited our allies to join us. They brought environmental concerns to the table, and together we discussed how we could support one another and work collectively to address environmental challenges and protect our Waters.

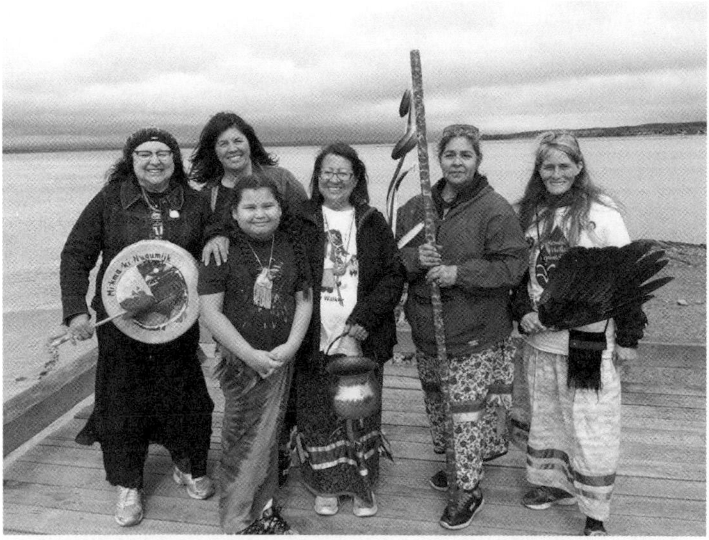

Mi'kmaki Water Walkers at the touchdown on Shubenacadie River. Patsy Stephens, Donna Stephens, Dorene Bernard, granddaughter Zahara Bernard, Carol Ducie Howe, Marian Nicholas.

---

On Victoria Day in 2007, we began the first Water Walk in Point Pleasant Park in Halifax at Black Rock Beach with our All Nations Drum Group. For seven years, people came, brought friends, and walked and prayed for the Water, for healing and protection, to educate about the sacredness of Water, and to give thanks for the Water. The Mother Earth Water Walks brought greater awareness of the sacredness of Water and the need to continue Water Walk ceremonies everywhere on Mother Earth to protect the Water, pray for the Water, and keep teaching about the responsibility all people share to care for it. Many women have learned to lead Water Walks and continue Grandmother Josephine's legacy.

In 2015, we began offering more teachings, and

the Mi'kmaki Water Walk ceremony focused on the Shubenacadie River watershed and the immediate threats to the Water. As we worked to protect our river from the actions of governments and the Alton Gas project, the Grassroots Grandmothers spoke for the Water and the threatened lands. Our work became a ceremony as we carried our responsibilities to protect the Waters for future generations.

We have walked for the Water across Mi'kmaki and Wabanaki for the past 11 years and will continue, as proponents continue to arrive with plans to mine, extract, frack, and impact the Water, and we must protect it. From these experiences, the teachings of Water protection became even clearer to me: Water is sacred, ceremony is responsibility, and protecting the Water is inseparable from protecting our people.

## Water Protection and Water Walking in Mi'kma'ki

### *The Sacredness of Water*

Water is life. In Mi'kmaq teachings, Water is sacred, it is a living being, it has a spirit and is connected to all Creation. Across Mi'kma'ki, Water protection is not only an environmental responsibility — it is a spiritual, cultural, and ancestral duty carried forward through ceremony, prayer, and action.

### *The Role of Women and Water Walkers*

The Water Walk Ceremony has become an important expression of women's responsibilities. Inspired by the late Grandmother Josephine Mandamin and the Mother Earth Water Walk, which brought Indigenous women and Water Protectors together across Turtle Island, these ceremonies are acts of prayer, love, gratitude, respect, and advocacy for the Water. As Water Protectors and Grassroots Grandmothers, we learned from Grandmother Josephine, our mentor, Elder, and friend, and from our Elders about our responsibilities as women, Water Walkers, and Water Protectors.

Participants walk alongside rivers, lakes, coastlines, and waterways, following a leader carrying a copper pail of Water and an eagle staff while offering songs and prayers for healing and protection. The walks remind communities that Water is alive and must be treated with respect.

### *Environmental Racism*

Water protection today also means speaking out against pollution, over-development, and environmental destruction that threaten the health of the land, the Waters, and all life that depends on them. We call this Environmental Racism, where the lands and Waters of unceded Mi'kmaki are threatened by development, resource extraction, mining, and fracking planned without the involvement of Mi'kmaq people.

When we are not informed of these plans, when government permits are issued to destroy the environment, when we are not consulted about our responsibilities to the lands and Waters, and when our consent is not obtained, there is always an impact—an impact on our Treaty Rights, Inherent Rights, and on our unceded Mi'kmaq lands, Waters, and people.

### *Future Generations*

Many Elders and Water Protectors emphasize that protecting Water is inseparable from protecting future generations. The teachings remind us that decisions made today must consider their impact on the next seven generations. The teaching of Netukulimk is to honour the environment, the land, Water, medicines, and all life for providing what we need to sustain ourselves, while taking only what we need and protecting the integrity of the environment so there will always be enough for the next seven generations.

### *Ceremony and Relationship*

The Water walks are powerful acts of ceremony. Each one begins with a sacred pipe ceremony. Each step is taken with intention. Songs are sung for the Water and tobacco is offered. People walk through sun, rain, wind, and exhaustion because the Water itself cannot speak in human language — the people become its voice. The relationship between the people and the Water is strengthened.

At the heart of Water protection is relationship and ceremony. The Mi'kmaq understanding is not that humans own the Water, but that we belong to the

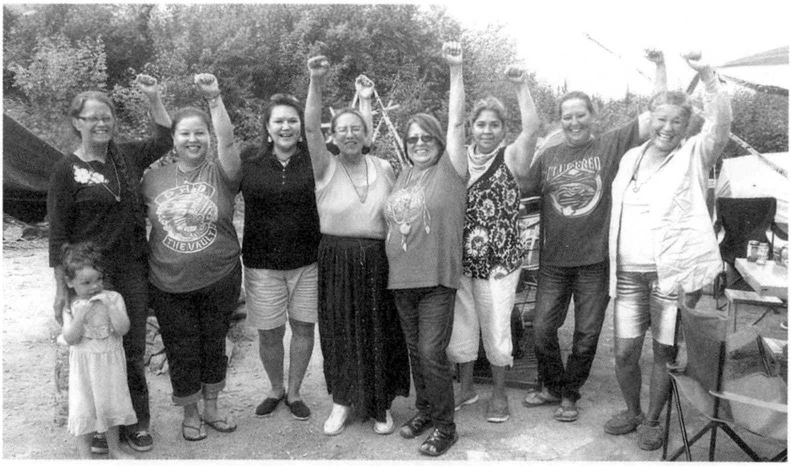

Wabanaki Water Protectors at Stop Sisson Mine Camp. Mary Reed, (child, not named), Ramona Nicholas, Jacinda Mack, Hart Perley, Dorene Bernard, Ducie Howe, Terry Sappier and Beverly Perley.

---

Water. The rivers and oceans have carried the stories, prayers, and lives of the people since time immemorial. Through Water Walking, those relationships are renewed, especially each spring, when the cycle of renewal and rebirth reminds us of our responsibilities. As an Elder or Water Protector might say, "When we protect the Water, we protect ourselves. The Water remembers our ancestors, and it carries life to those yet unborn." In Mi'kmaq, we say, Nin tela'teketes wujit Samqwan — I will do it for the Water.

Water Walking in Mi'kma'ki continues to bring together Elders, youth, families, and allies in ceremony and collective responsibility. It is both a reminder and a call to action: the Water must remain clean, respected, and free for future generations.

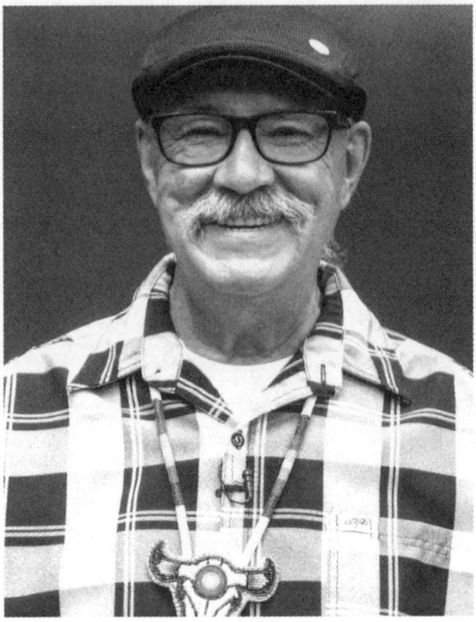

## EUGENE ARCAND

Eugene Arcand, a Cree from Muskeg Lake First Nation, attended St. Michael Indian Residential School and St. Paul's Lebret Students Residence in Saskatchewan. A First Nations Sports Hall of Fame inductee, he has devoted decades to organizing sports, cultural, tourism, and youth events. Through the TRC Survivor Committee and NCTR Governing Circle, he has helped keep Survivors and the public informed about the Residential School Settlement Agreement.

# My Life with Hockey

By Eugene Arcand

## The Saving Grace of 'Blameless Shame'

When I got out of residential school at the age of 17, I didn't give a shit about anyone or anything. I was filled with hate.

It was nothing for me to get into all sorts of conflicts with the Settler community, including the police, for no reason. I was afraid of nothing. I had no fear. I had just done 11 years of hard time. You want to send me to jail again? Fine, I don't give a shit. That was the mentality and psychology I had. So, I went on a three-year binge of booze, drugs — anything I could ingest. I never put on a pair of skates during those first three years after residential school.

Then, at the age of 20, this incredible lady, my wife Lorna, came into my life. She was 18 and we were married in 1972. I don't know how she put up with me, because for the next 15 to 20 years, I was still being a piss tank, a druggie, a scrapper. I lived two lives — the life of a dangerously dysfunctional person and the life of an athlete.

For a long time in our marriage, I never shared with Lorna any of the stories I'm sharing here. Once in a while I might say this or that happened but never to any great extent. I carried shame for having experienced deviant behaviour with adults, members of the clergy and other perverts who worked in those residential schools. It was not just me. I know today who abused who and when it happened. And I know how damaging it was to all those kids. And they know the same about me. We don't talk about it in that graphic way. We just know we were traumatized children, who are damaged goods today. We are just trying to fix ourselves.

So, after Lorna came into my life, I tried to straighten out, but I still didn't really know how to love. I didn't know how to grieve. I didn't know how to hug. I was just this rank guy trying to survive in a world that was not normal to me. The only thing that felt normal to me was being on the ice, the soccer field, the rugby field, a volleyball court, or basketball court.

Sports were my safe space. But then there was the reality of life. It didn't take long for us to start having children. I had to adapt into that world of trying to work to support my family and still play sports. Most of my work was minimum wage. I washed dishes, piled cement blocks, I was a night watchman, but I was still leading a totally dysfunctional lifestyle.

Even well into my 30s, after 15 years of marriage, I still hadn't really shared much of my trauma with Lorna. I gave her every reason to kick me out or leave me. But she stuck with me. I'm lucky she did. I thought I would end up in a maximum-security prison at some point or that I wouldn't live to see today. That's where I was headed, and I had no fear of it.

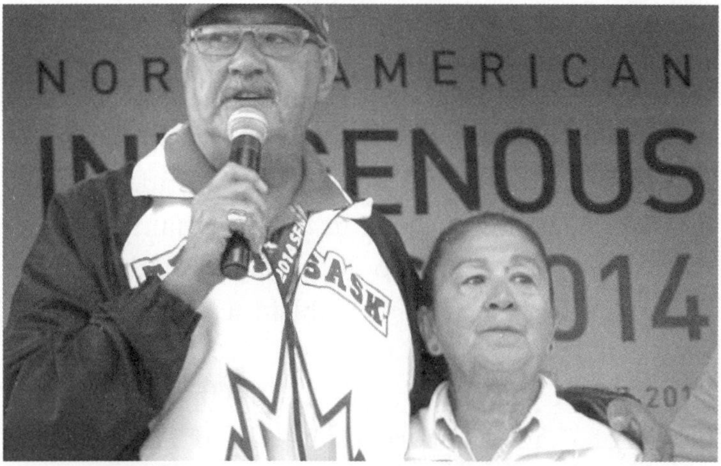


My wife Lorna and I working on behalf of the North American Indigenous Games. *(Eagle Feather News)*

One day, a friend of mine asked me to go to the University of Saskatchewan to listen to a guest speaker. I reluctantly went. I had a hangover. I didn't want to be there. I knew I didn't fit in at any academic institution. But I went. This lecturer was talking about "blameless shame." It's important, he said, to understand this blameless shame. I was at the very back of the auditorium and my light went on.

I remember leaving the university and thinking, *Everything that guy said was about me. I've been carrying this shame around and didn't even realize it was shame.* Blameless shame is when you realize you've done nothing wrong; it's when you realize you were not the pervert who sexually, physically and psychologically abused kids. We were just innocent children who were molested and abused. I had a hard time coming to terms with that part of my life. I was filled with so much hatred.

When I began accepting the concept of blameless shame, I started on my journey of healing. Then I started sharing it with my fellow residential school survivors and other people in our communities who needed to hear it. I'd say to them, "You hear about this thing blameless shame?" I'd explain it to them. Their eyes would go big.

I started getting reacquainted with myself between the age of 35 and 40. It was a slow transition; I was still an addict. I'd go five or six days sober, something would happen, and off the deep end I would go. I never went to rehab. I'd battle it on my own. Even when I was wild in my mid-30s, I could still perform athletically. I was still running track in my 30s; I was still playing soccer. I was 6-foot-3 and 210 pounds. I was sinewy. I think it's another reason I'm alive today. I played hard in my life in so many negative ways, but I trained hard too. I lifted weights. I was big, strong, fast, agile. By the time I was 40, I was starting to figure out some things.

When I got out of residential school, I had no idea how good an athlete I was. None of us did, even though we would often beat and dominate Settler teams in a lot of school sports. We didn't know what we didn't know, eh?

Once I was married, my wife and I went through life surviving as best we could. Thankfully, my wife took care of the family when I was absent; when I was gone for a week at a time, her not knowing if I was alive because I was disappearing from the realities of life.

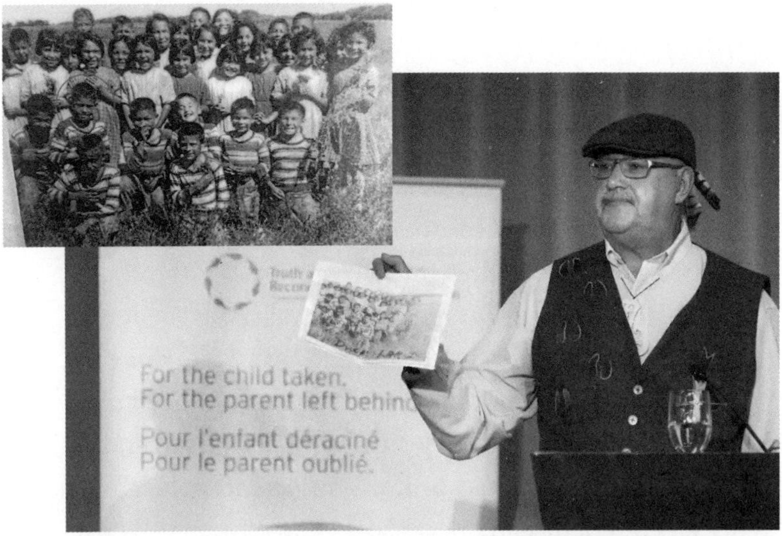


With a photo of my St. Michael's Residential School classmates.
Classmates picture is shown upper left.

---

As out of control as much of my life was, by the age of 23 I was back playing hockey regularly; first in the Commercial League as well as some Indigenous tournaments and events. Between 1975 and 1981, I played for the North Battleford Beaver Blues in the Saskatchewan Intermediate AAA League, high-level senior/semi-pro hockey against teams that were competing to win the Allan Cup (emblematic of national senior amateur hockey champions).

As a hockey player, I can say I was never treated as well as I was by the Blues. I am forever grateful for that. It was the first time in my life, where if you needed skates, you got new skates. If you needed gloves, you got them. You got everything you needed. You would get five dozen sticks to start the season. We even had our names on our sticks. That Blues organization treated me with so much respect. It was the first time in my life that I felt genuinely accepted in Settler society.

I can also say I was treated horribly by opposing players and fans at that time. I was usually the only First Nations player on the team. I was often the only First Nations player in the league. And the rinks I visited, when they folded up the sticks after the game was over, the only one they didn't fold up was Arcand's stick. They knew I had to use it to defend myself on my way out of the rink because there were people who wanted to kill the Indian. So, I didn't only experience it as a child at residential school; I experienced it as an adult athlete. There's nothing you can think of that wasn't said or done to me. I've experienced it all.

If you've seen the movie *Indian Horse*, everything that happened to the lead character, Saul, happened to me. I was threatened and assaulted — not just on the ice either. I had no desire to club any person over the head; I had no thirst to hurt someone. But if I was threatened and in danger, I was fearless and ruthless. I can't say I'm proud of those moments, but I will not apologize for any of my actions. The residential school system created a monster.

I was spit on; I had stuff thrown on me. It's happened to my wife when they found out she was at my game. They would spit in her coffee. When it's done to me, I can deal with it. But when it's done to my people, I can't accept that. And it's still happening today.

I will go to a AAA midget hockey game in Saskatchewan, and I hear some of the Settler parents, the slurs they are hurling at children they've never met in their lives. They've never met the First Nations players' parents. They don't know if those parents are employed or if they're trying to be a positive part of society. And the First Nations players and their parents are called down like dogs. Spit on. Abused like dogs. And who tries to stop it from happening? No one. If someone does come to enforce it, who do you think will get charged? Who'll be the one in trouble? Me and my people, that's who. I say this from experience. I'm not crying on your shoulder. This is real life.

On the other hand, as an adult athlete playing with and against Settlers, other players would come up to me and say, "Where did you learn to play like that?" and "Where did you play junior?" I wouldn't answer. I would be on a ball field, whacking them out, playing great defence and they would come up to me and say, "Where did you learn to play fastball?" I wouldn't answer them. I played centre half in soccer — I played in the first ever Saskatchewan Summer Games in Moose Jaw in 1972 and people would come up to me and ask, "Where did you learn to play soccer?" I wouldn't answer them. That's because I didn't want to say residential school. I didn't understand shame, the shame of residential school.

I didn't learn mental toughness in a way it should ever be learned. I learned mental toughness in residential school. My mental toughness carried me through sports as an adult athlete. And now it carries me through my work when I speak to people about my life for the sake of public education. I prepare the same way: give my all for as long as it takes to get the job done. I go full bore.

I played my sports rough. I never held back. I handled myself okay. If they started getting the best of me in a fight, I would do whatever I needed to in order to survive — pulling hair, scratching, biting, gouging — there isn't anything I wouldn't do. Usually when I would see them again, they didn't want to go anymore. I didn't win them all, but I made sure they didn't want to fight again.

I was targeted a lot. I recall on a number of occasions being called on in the first period. I'd tell them, "I don't want to fight right now, we'll go later. Let's play hockey for a while." They would call me a chicken shit. That was fine, but I made sure by the time the third period came along, and we had a lead, I'd remind them of the offer. Most times they didn't want anything to do with me. You have to know how to handle yourself. It was survival skills.

It wasn't easy. There were times I wanted to quit hockey. I couldn't handle the racism. Every weekend I'd go to these arenas; it was not a nice experience. The hockey was good. But the behaviour of people in Saskatchewan towards me was what I call normalized horrible.

I would call a friend of mine, my mentor, Ray Ahenakew. Ray was in the generation of Indian hockey players in Saskatchewan who came after Freddy Sasakamoose but before me. Ray played for the Yorkton Terriers and for a lot of senior intermediate leagues. People in our communities still talk about the fight he once had with former NHL/CFL player Gerry James.

Ray knew what I was experiencing. I'd tell him, "I can't do it anymore. I can't handle this shit anymore." He told me, "You can't quit, buddy. You've made it to this level, and you have to keep going because if you quit, they're going to pass judgment on the rest of us." And how true his words became. So, I always tried to stick it out. I faced all my suspensions. I faced all the strategic moves that were designed to slow me down or cool me down. I've tried to live by that, as best I could, in the rest of my life, too.

And I'd fight back as best I could, try to stand up for myself and my People.

Before games, I wouldn't rise and stand up for the Canadian national anthem. I did it because of the treatment of my People. When NFL quarterback Colin Kaepernick first kneeled during the American national anthem to highlight racial injustice in 2016, my friend Richard Mirasty, a very well-respected criminal defence attorney in Alberta, reminded me I was doing it in the 1970s. I remember one time in particular, our coach on the Blues, Merv Borgeson, told me I better stand for the anthem or the referees might give us a penalty. I told him to forget about it, because it wasn't happening. He kept on me about it and I told him, "If you want me to stand up, I'll walk out of this rink right now and you'll never see me again." He never said another word.

I had some really good coaches with the Blues. Bobby Sheppard, (former NHL forward) Gregg Sheppard's brother, was one of them. Merv was another. I recall one time when Merv rearranged the lines. He had put me on a line with a couple of players who I viewed as closet rednecks. As we were getting ready to go on the ice, Merv said, "Everyone ready to go?" I told him, "I'm not ready to go. I don't want to play on that line." And it was the first line. He said, "Why not, Arcand? What's the problem?" I told him, "I don't want to play on a line and have to protect people I don't trust. I can't protect people I don't trust. Put me on another line."

That really affected the dressing room, but I was not going to put up with that kind of shit. I was being honest and truthful. Sure, those guys are my teammates, but I also knew some of the things they had said over the course of the years I had played with them. They had to pay their dues back with me before I was going to step up for them. Because when I had to step up for my team and my teammates, I would really step up. I was not a person to start brawls, but if someone was going after my linemates, I'd step up for them.

I liked the line I played on, with two Ukrainian guys, Pat, who went by the nickname Hoyo, and Lionel, who went by Weenie. They were good guys. I liked and respected them. They both could score goals, but they needed someone to go into the corners and do the dirty work. That was my job. I'm feeling for them right now because they're both Ukrainian. It's so horrible what's going on there with Russia.

I made many friends in hockey, both Settlers and Indigenous. I think of my time playing and I think of Gazoo, Dickie, Snazz, Chaboy, Guy, Bruce '7', Greg, Porky, Floppy, Howie, Joey, Eddy, Dale, Tubby, Midge, Albert M, Moe, Filthy, Ron, Louis, Ovide, Abe... and so many more.

My last year with the Blues was in 1981; I was getting close to 30 years old. I'd had enough. I still played lower-level hockey on and off until I was 40 but once I started to get my life more in order, between 35 and 40, there were other things for me. My wife and family was one; reconnecting with my culture and getting back what was lost and taken away from me when I went to residential school was another.

**Finding My Heroes**

Residential school took away so much from me, but it was there, at Duck Lake as a small boy, I found my heroes.

I remember being only seven or eight years old when I saw a film about Jim Thorpe and the Carlisle Indian School, in Carlisle, Pennsylvania. Thorpe had attended that school before going on to become an Olympian and one of the greatest athletes in the world. He was a hero to me.

Another one of my heroes was Gordie Howe. I remember being at St. Michael's and on Saturday night we would all sit around and watch *Hockey Night in Canada* on this little black and white TV. All the kids would cheer for the Toronto Maple Leafs or Montreal Canadiens, but I didn't like either one of those teams.

I heard the commentators talking about this young hockey player from Saskatoon, Saskatchewan, on the Detroit Red Wings and his name was Gordie Howe. I knew nothing about him, but from that moment forward, because he was from Saskatoon, he was a hero to me. Years later, when I got to see Gordie play, I loved him even more because he played hockey the way I wanted to play the game.

My Number 1 hero was Fred Sasakamoose, a Cree hockey player from the Ahtahkakoop Cree Nation. I actually had heard stories about Fred at home at a very young age, before I went to St. Michael's, from my grandparents.

When I arrived at Duck Lake, I learned that Fred had attended St. Michael's before me and learned to play hockey there. He went on to play for the Chicago Blackhawks in the 1953-54 season and become the first First Nations (with treaty status) player in the NHL. We heard all about his great athletic accomplishments — not only his hockey exploits, but also in soccer and his incredible speed in track and field. When he was a little guy, they said nobody could catch him — on the ice or the field or the track. Freddy became my hero from those stories.

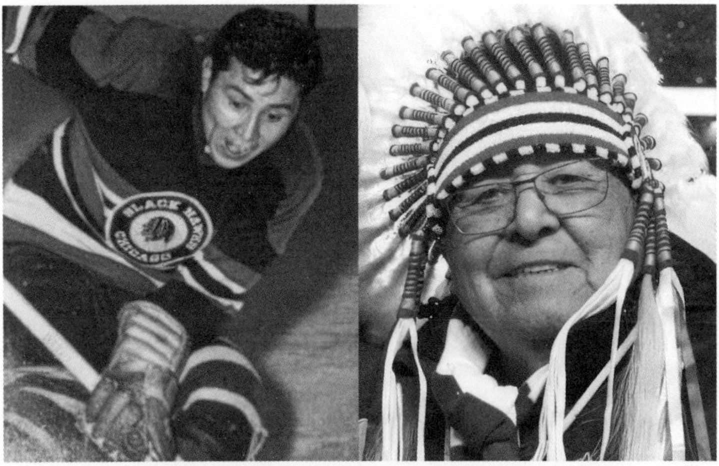

Fred Sasakamoose, as a Chicago Blackhawk
and a Cree Nation Chief.

It's still amazing to me that I not only got to meet my heroes, both Gordie and Fred, but become close with them, especially Fred.

I'll never forget the first time I met Fred. I was probably 16 or 17 years old, towards the end of my time in residential school, and it was Easter break. There was a big Indian tourney in North Battleford — in its heyday it was the Stanley Cup of Indian hockey. I was injured and up in the stands watching my team play. My buddy was carrying the puck up the ice and there was a guy in the stands who said, "Who's that guy? He's a helluva skater." I asked someone, "Who is that guy [asking the question]?" and they said, "That's Fred Sasakamoose."

I made my way over to him. He said to me, "You play hockey?"

I said, "Yeah, with these guys on the ice."

"Why aren't you out there?" he asked me.

"I'm injured," I told him. "My knee is banged up."

Fred looked at me and I'll never forget what he said: "Long way from the heart, kid."

That's what he said to me. I adopted that. For the rest of the time I played hockey, I was never carried off the ice. I always skated off. No matter how hurt I was, how beaten up I was, I'd get myself off the ice.

That was my first experience with Fred. I didn't get to know him better until years later. I got to see him play some games in his later years in Saskatchewan. We worked together to promote sports, recreation and culture for Indigenous kids. And we became close friends.

Fred making the NHL was an amazing accomplishment. The fact he played a small number of games (11) in the NHL has been trivialized recently. Anyone who would do that, well, they have no idea. There were only 120 players in the six-team league at that time. For anyone to make it, even for one game, is unbelievable.

But for Freddie to have been in a residential school and go through everything he had to deal with in his life, to get to The Show, even for a cup of coffee... Freddie went through hell to be the MVP of the Western Hockey League; he went through hell to get to the NHL. Most people have no idea. And I don't know what happened, why Freddie didn't play more games, but something happened.

When Fred went to Chicago in November of 2002 to be honoured by the Blackhawks, he asked me to go along with him. I've never talked publicly about what I heard and saw that day.

We were in owner Bill Wirtz's office. His son, William Wirtz Jr., was there, too. William Jr. had given us a nice tour of the United Centre. And there was another person in the office, a little old man with white hair. I don't know his name. This man whispered something to Bill Wirtz. Then Bill whispered something to his son. I don't know what was said, but the little old man with white hair, and I could hear him, said: "Come on Bill, you know damn well that what happened to Freddie here was not right."

Bill Wirtz then opened up his desk drawer and pulled out a small square box. He opened it up and it was this large fine-cut diamond with the Blackhawks' logo on top of it, celebrating the franchise's 75th anniversary. He gave that box to Fred. The little old man with the white hair then said to Fred, "Only 75 of those were ever made."

I later asked Fred about what the man had said in the office, about something that happened to him. A couple of times, actually, but Fred would just shake his head and say nothing. He didn't want to talk about it. But something happened.

Fred died in hospital on Nov. 24, 2020, after getting Covid. He was 86. He was such an inspiration to our People, not only for making it to the NHL but for all he did after that. He worked with young people, promoting sport, in our communities. He was a band councilor and Chief of the Ahtahkakoop. He testified about his time at a residential school to the Truth and Reconciliation Committee. He was my friend; he was my hero.

The first time I met Gordie Howe was thanks to my friend Gerry Nelson, who is one of the top blind golfers in the world. When I was in North Battleford, I got to know Gerry. He was a rare cat, a little blonde Settler guy who liked hanging out with Indigenous People. Before he lost his sight because of diabetes, we played hockey and ball and hung out whenever we could. His nickname with us with is Sniveler.

You might have heard of Gerry and his son Wyatt. In 2016, their story got national coverage because Wyatt would do play-by-play for his dad while sitting beside Gerry at Saskatoon Blades games. The St. Louis Blues invited them to an NHL game. They got to spend time with the Stanley Cup and Wyatt did some play-by-play for his dad on the Blues' radio broadcast of that game.

So, Gerry invited me to play in a Canadian National Institute for the Blind (CNIB) fundraising golf tourney in Saskatoon and Gordie Howe was there as an ambassador for the CNIB. Gordie was at the 10th hole, signing autographs and getting his picture taken. Gerry and Gordie already knew each other. Gerry introduced me to Gordie, and I told Gordie he was one of two heroes in my life, Fred Sasakamoose being the other.

Gordie looked me in the eye and told me it was an honour to meet me. He had no idea who he was talking to, but I knew who I was talking to. A few minutes later, we had to line up for pictures. Just before the first picture was being taken, I said to Gerry, "Sniv, I know you're blind but you're facing the wrong way." So, I turned him around. Gordie is looking at me like, "What the hell are you doing?" So, with Gerry now facing the wrong way, we took the picture. I turned Sniv back around, we all had a good laugh and then took a proper picture. Gordie was shaking his head, he said to me, "You're a real character, aren't you?" That was the beginning of a friendship. We met up at the banquet after the golf and spent some time together.

We would run into each other over the course of a number of years, the last of which was at former NHL players Garry Peters' and Rich Pilon's charity golf tourney. Gordie was so tickled at us playing a joke on our blind friend that he always remembered me. It was a really hot day and Gordie was at that age when he was starting to need some help with things, so his son, Marty, was with him.

When we got to the tee box where Gordie and Marty were, Marty mentioned what a nice day it would be if they were golfing instead of standing around in the hot sun. I jumped right on that: "Well, Marty, I got a good set of clubs here. Why don't you jump on the cart and finish the round? I'll sit with your Dad." So, Gordie and I spent the afternoon together. It was a dream for me. A few hours with Gordie. When hockey people get together, not a lot has to be said. It just feels good. He felt good with me there and I felt good with him there. We shared some funny things, but I also shared some stories from my life, and he shared some of his stories, too.

One of the things that Gordie said to me that day was, "Freddy [Sasakamoose] didn't get a fair shake in Chicago." That stayed with me for the rest of time. And that was the second time someone who knew about Fred's time in Chicago had mentioned something happening. For Gordie to say that about Freddy, it really meant something. Gordie had the longest career in hockey, but he knew all about Freddy's short career. And how relevant was it for my two heroes to be connected like that?

**Big Bird, That's Me**

I can also thank hockey for giving me my nickname: "Big Bird," which then got shortened to Bird. I was playing in a tourney at Onion Lake on the Alberta/Saskatchewan border when I was around 20 years old. I always wore No. 14. We were playing the Onion Lake Border Chiefs in Seekaskootch Arena and my nemesis on that team was a little fireplug, the late Randy Whitestone. My job was to slow him down. He was a local favourite. If you touched him, the crowd would go nuts. I would go after him hard.

There was a break in the action and there was this lady, the late Anna Crowe, who was Randy's auntie. So, she stands up and yells at me: "No. 14, you asshole! I hate you, you big...." She paused, maybe because she realized everyone was looking at her or maybe she didn't want to swear again. And then she said: "You big bird!" All the fans laughed. That was the start of my nickname and it stuck.

I always say hockey is a small world. I love being around hockey people, just talking and sharing stories. I remember one sports dinner at the Dakota Dunes Casino where Bryan Trottier, Bob Bourne, and Clark Gillies made an appearance.

They asked Trots who he wanted to look after them, to host them at the dinner, and he said, "Big Bird." Trots and I knew each other from some Indigenous events. Clark Gillies and Bobby Bourne were Saskatchewan guys who played junior in Regina and Saskatoon.

The night of the banquet, there was an autograph session. There was a long lineup to get their autographs. A Settler wearing a farmer's cap came up to me and shook my hand. "How you doing, Big Bird?" I couldn't place him. He seemed to know me so well. He didn't get in the autograph line, but he kept asking me to get him to the front to get autographs and pictures with the players.

After the banquet is over, there's a lineup to talk to the players. This farmer guy is about tenth in line. He calls me over and says, "Big Bird, get me up there. You're the guy here. Make it happen." I told him, "Relax, partner. You'll get your shot." He kept bugging me and I finally got fed up and told him to wait his turn and that everyone else is waiting, too. And then I said, "Besides, I don't even know you."

He said, "You don't remember me? Well, maybe you will remember this," and he took off his hat. I suddenly remembered who he was. So, I said, "Come with me, my friend." I didn't know his name but now I knew who he was. So, I get him up there with the players and he rats me out to Trots, Gillies, and Bourne. "You see this scar on my head?" he asked them. "Big Bird did this to me and I wasn't even on the ice."

It's a pretty funny story.

Back in the day, I was playing for the intermediate Blues in a game at Unity. There was no plexiglass back then; it was all chicken wire. I went into the corner, got turned around and got hit a couple of times. My stick went through the chicken wire into the stands and a Settler fan grabs my stick.

Play goes down the ice, but he won't let go of my stick and he's really putting on a show. All the other Settlers are laughing. I realized brawn was not going to work because he was not going to let go. He was enjoying his celebrity too much. Finally, I said, "C'mon buddy, let my stick go. I gotta get down the ice." Surprisingly, he lets go. As soon as he did, I conked him over the head and took off down the ice.

The next shift I come out and there's a first-aid person there and they're patching up his forehead. He's leaking pretty bad. And they left a big chunk of cotton batting taped on his forehead. So, I see this, I point at him and start laughing. That made all the other Settlers laugh. He's mad as hell but he can't do anything about it.

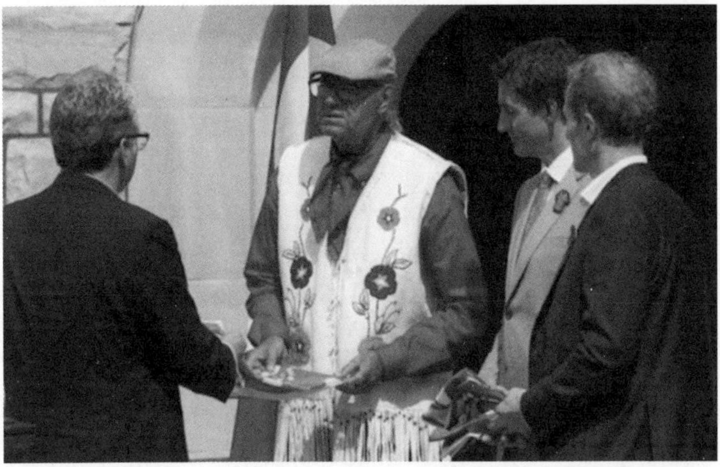

It was a battle to get the Survivors' flag on Parliament Hill but we have raised it now four years in a row.

---

So, I kept it going the whole game. I would skate down the ice with the puck and make-believe I was going to shoot it at him. And that made the fans go even more crazy. Then he would go crazy.

Well, fair to say Trots, Clark, and Bobby loved that story.

There aren't many spaces in this world where I feel truly comfortable. Being with my people, fellow survivors, is definitely the most important one, but being with hockey people is another.

• • •

"My Life in Hockey" has been adapted from "781: A Story of Sports and Survival," an interview with Eugene Arcand developed and produced by Bob MacKenzie for The Sports Network (TSN).

# The History of the National Centre for Truth and Reconciliation: A Survivor's Perspective

By Eugene Arcand

ONE OF THE BIGGEST MISCONCEPTIONS about the National Centre for Truth and Reconciliation is that it somehow appeared out of nowhere. It did not. To understand the Centre, you have to go back to the work of the Truth and Reconciliation Commission. When the Commission completed its work, it left behind more than a report. It left behind a roadmap in the form of the 94 Calls to Action, the United Nations Declaration on the Rights of Indigenous Peoples, and the Principles of Reconciliation. The National Centre grew out of that work.

What many people do not know is that when the Truth and Reconciliation Commission presented its final report in Ottawa, there was no permanent home for its legacy. The National Centre was, in a very real sense, homeless. Along with my friend John Morrisseau, I served on the Survivor Circle that worked with the Commission. When the Commission concluded, we were left with the Bentwood Box, the Eagle Staff, and other sacred ceremonial objects, but nowhere to house them. Ryan Moran worked with us to find a temporary home at the Canadian Museum for Human Rights in Winnipeg, which cared for these sacred items until the Centre was established.

At the same time, Chancellor's Hall at the University of Manitoba was being renovated. Some people described it as haunted. We explained that from our perspective it was spiritually occupied. That distinction matters. Residential schools taught many of us to view our own beliefs through a colonial lens. Some people call the journey back healing. I call it wellness. Wellness means relearning who we are and seeing the world through Indigenous ways of knowing rather than through the conditioning imposed on us.

In those early years, our relationship with the University of Manitoba was very much a hat-in-hand relationship. Several Indigenous institutions across Canada had hoped to host the Centre, and there were strong feelings after the decision was made. The original Call to Action referred to a National Research Centre, but we chose the name National Centre for Truth and Reconciliation because truth was, and remains, the most important word.

As a Residential School Survivor, I still ask: What the hell are we reconciling? What did we do wrong? Too often people rush to reconciliation without first facing the truth. The Centre was never created to make Canadians feel better about the past. It was created to preserve the truth about what happened and to ensure future generations would have access to that truth.

Although the National Centre is located at

the University of Manitoba, it does not belong to the University. It belongs to Residential School Survivors and our descendants. It safeguards some of our darkest truths, and there have been ongoing attempts to challenge or control those truths. One of the most significant battles involved the preservation of Independent Assessment Process records. Under a Supreme Court ruling, those records can be destroyed unless Survivors request that they be preserved.

I want my records preserved. I have nothing to hide. I was not the one who committed the abuse. If my grandchildren and great-grandchildren want to know what happened to me, I want them to have access to that truth. That is why the National Centre matters. It exists to protect our stories and ensure that what happened to us is never forgotten.

**Protecting What Belongs to Survivors**

Over time, our relationship with the University of Manitoba has improved because there is now a better understanding that the Centre is an autonomous institution. It belongs to Residential School Survivors and our descendants. It is not a government institution or an academic institution. It is a Survivor institution.

The Centre safeguards some of our darkest truths, and those truths have often been

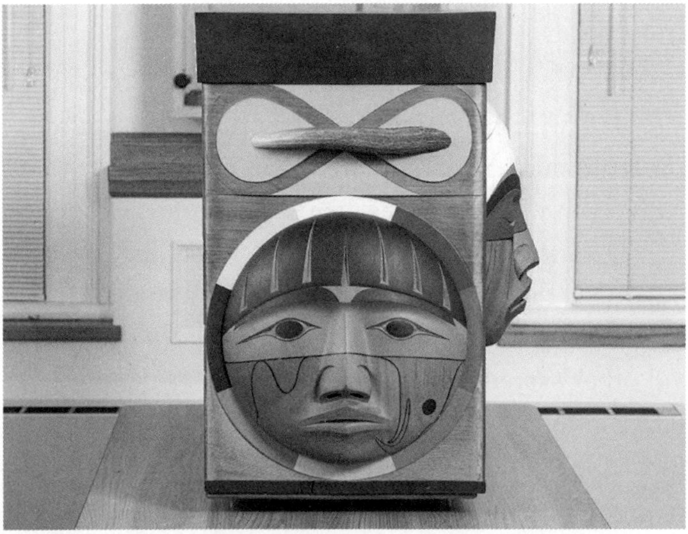

The Bentwood Box: Coast Salish artist Luke Marston created the box from a single piece of sacred, old-growth red cedar.

challenged. One of the most difficult chapters in our history involved attempts to discredit the Centre's ability to protect Survivor records. The conflict eventually reached the Supreme Court of Canada and raised serious concerns about the future of Independent Assessment Process records. Many of us fought to ensure that Survivors would have the option to preserve their testimonies for future generations. I want my records preserved. I want my children, grandchildren, and great-grandchildren to know what happened.

Another challenge has been correcting the public record. For years, discussions about abuse in residential schools often focused on student-on-student abuse while overlooking the responsibility of clergy and staff who held power within those institutions. The truth matters, and the Centre exists to protect that truth, even when it makes people uncomfortable.

During our early years, we remained deeply grateful to the Canadian Museum for Human Rights, which cared for the Bentwood Box, the Eagle Staff, and other sacred items while we established a permanent home. When those sacred objects were finally transferred to the National Centre, it was an emotional moment. It reminded all of us that these are not simply artifacts. They carry our history, our ceremonies, and our responsibilities.

As Survivors, we inherited the National Centre much like we inherit a child or a grandchild. It must be nurtured and protected. During the first six years, that responsibility weighed heavily on many of us. The Centre lived in poverty. We constantly struggled for funding and often worried about keeping the doors open. I served as Chair during those years, and they were among the most difficult of my adult life.

Everything changed after the discovery of the 215 children at Kamloops. Public awareness increased, governments paid attention, and support for the Centre grew. Yet new challenges also emerged. Consultants, researchers, and businesses suddenly appeared, claiming expertise in residential school investigations and unmarked graves. Some helped communities, but others profited from our grief and

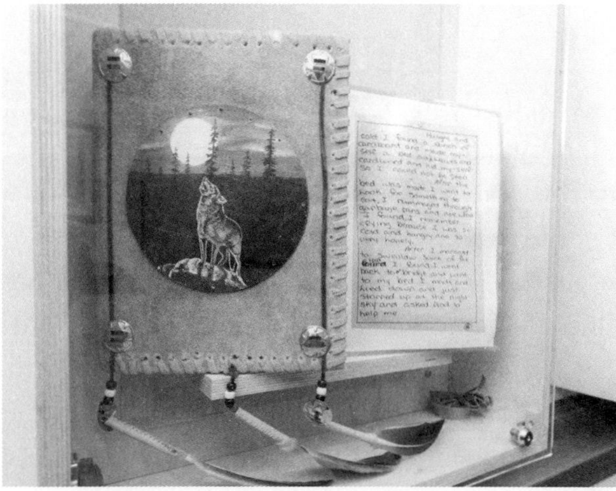

Leather-bound book adorned with eagle feathers, containing the handwritten diary of Stanley Normand from Sagkeeng First Nation, a Survivor of Fort Alexander Indian Residential School.

presented themselves as experts on experiences they had never lived.

That is why the National Centre remains so important. It ensures that Survivors remain the caretakers of our own history. Our stories, our records, our sacred objects, and our truths belong to us and to the generations that follow.

### The Centre Is Our Grandchild

The National Centre for Truth and Reconciliation did not simply appear one day. It was built by Residential School Survivors and Indigenous Peoples. It carries some of our darkest truths and reflects the long-term impacts of residential schools on our families and communities.

Whether you are First Nations, Inuit, or Métis, so many of the challenges we continue to face can be traced back to a policy designed to take the Indian out of the child.

At the same time, our goal has always been wellness. People often talk about healing, but I prefer the word wellness. For many Survivors, that journey is still ongoing. I only learned how to cry in the last fifteen years. Many of us were taught as children not to cry, not to show emotion, and not to speak about what happened to us. Those lessons followed us into adulthood and, in some cases, into our parenting. We passed on behaviours we did not fully understand because they had been passed on to us. We cannot change that history, but we can talk about it and learn from it.

That is one reason the National Centre matters so much. I often describe it as our grandchild. We have inherited it, and we must nurture it. One day it will stand long after we are gone, preserving our stories, our truths, and the evidence of what really happened. It will hold the voices of people who were called lazy, savage, drunk, addicted, and broken. It will tell the truth about children who were taken from their families and subjected to policies that amounted to genocide.

This is your Centre. It is our Centre. Never allow anyone to convince you otherwise. It does not belong to governments or outside institutions. It belongs to Survivors and to future generations. One day we will bring our children and grandchildren there so they can learn the truth for themselves.

The truth cannot be sugar-coated. We are not sharing these stories to shame Canada or the churches. We are sharing them because what happened was wrong and because those truths were hidden for far too long. For many years, I carried a shame that never belonged to me. Over time, I came to understand the idea of blameless shame. I realized that I had done nothing wrong. We were not the people who harmed children. We were the children who were harmed.

That understanding changes everything. I encourage people to reconnect with their cultures, relearn their languages, and continue the journey toward wellness. Those are the foundations of truth, and they are the foundations upon which future generations will build.

The National Centre for Truth and Reconciliation exists to protect those truths. It belongs to Survivors, to our descendants, and to all those who are committed to ensuring that this history is never forgotten.

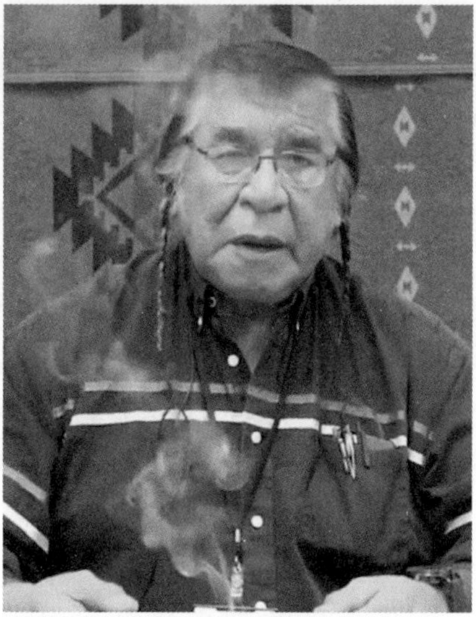

## KEITH CHIEFMOON

Keith Chiefmoon is a Ga'na (Kainai) Sundance teacher and Indian Residential School Program and Community Engagement worker with the Kainai Wellness Center, Blood Tribe Department of Health. A Survivor of both Catholic and Anglican residential schools, he later faced racism in public schools. Despite these hardships, he became addictions-free over 40 years ago and earned degrees in Native American Studies, Education, and Administration. Keith is a member of the Governing Circle of the NCTR.

PHOTO: HTTPS://WWW.YOUTUBE.COM/WATCH?V=OBWSR-6KGBA

# Nurturing

By Keith Chiefmoon

JUST THE OTHER DAY, I had a chance to look out into a field and witness the caring bond of a cow with her newborn calf. I also saw how the birds care for their young in the nest. What I saw was the way nature is loving and nurturing.

I was brought up by my parents until I was ten years old and even though they had both attended residential school they still knew how to care for us, giving us our morning hugs, speaking to us in our language, and always checking in with us to be sure we were doing okay.

My dad would sometimes take us down to the river to learn how to be respectful to the animals, particularly in the springtime. We would see the beavers making a dam and he'd tell us to be super quiet so we could watch them working. They had some little ones with them and we would see the mother leading the babies to show them how to build. Dad would say, "Unless you are super quiet, they will sound the alarm." We could see the bond that was there among the beavers and the nurturing law that was among them.

Sometimes my older brothers, Gus, Wilfred, Ed, and Jordon would run away from residential school. They would show up at home at two or three o'clock in the morning. Instead of my dad getting upset with them, he'd say to us, "Just go ahead and play." He was very happy to see them home even though he knew that the RCMP would show up with the priest and they'd be sent back.

Residential school was the opposite of nurturing. My parents had a hard time sending us there. My mother cried when it came my time to leave. She too had been a victim of the residential schools. I was afraid when she cried.

When I became a student at St. Paul's Indian Residential School, I remember hearing stories from my friends. Some of their parents could see the school from their front porch. In the mornings, they would look toward the building. One friend told me he could see his parents sitting at a small table, crying, but there was nothing anyone could do.

It was natural for us to want to see our parents. That is what children do. But when we cried, the nuns would come over and hit us on the head. It happened so often it became almost a daily routine.

• • •

In our traditional ways, we grew up with nurturing from Day One. When a baby is born, it is part of our tradition to hold a gathering for the baby at the sweat lodge. Knowledge keepers, Elders, and relatives bless the child from the Four Directions. Each participant — Grannies, Aunties, Uncles — prays with the child

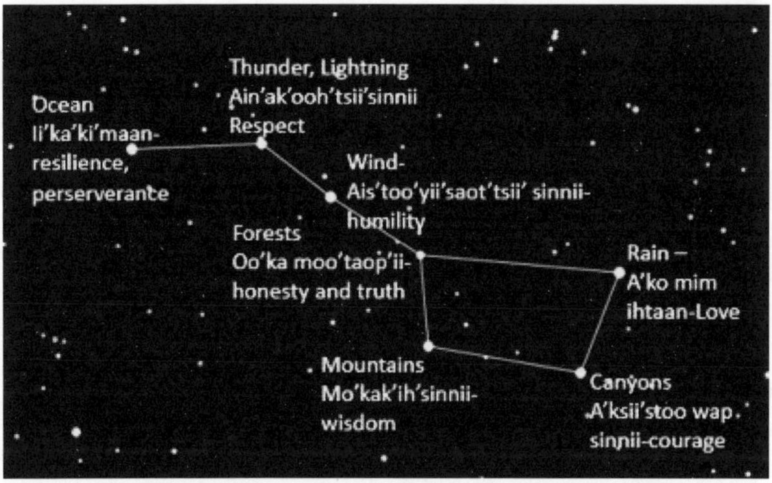


On a clear night, you can see the cosmic symbolism in the Big Dipper. The stars signify the Seven Sacred Gifts.

---

to survive in the world, giving a blessing for a good life. These honoured ceremonies of consensus reinforce the sharing of the values.

As we grow up, our parents teach us the responsibilities in the Niisitapi way of life. Symbolically, these responsibilities — our Blackfoot "Seven Sacred Gifts" — are represented on a clear night when you see the Big Dipper. Those stars are reminders telling us about forgiveness, love, compassion, not to be selfish, courage, respect, and understanding — all the Seven Sacred Gifts.

These gifts were severed when we were taken away to the residential school. They tried to force us to change our views. Instead of our traditional teachings, the school would use sticks to beat us and would use force for us to comprehend what they were talking about and to comply with their rules. It was an enormous contrast to our true family life.

When the sun comes up in the morning, it shines off every human being, whether you are Caucasian, Asian, Black, or First Nations, blessing us with a new day and telling us, "Remember the sacred teachings." Let me tell you now about the Seven Sacred Teachings you can see in the sun and stars.

**Love:** Love is the first thing we are given. I remember my parents giving us hugs in the morning, making sure we were okay. That is how you know you belong. Love is not something you have to earn. It is something you are born into. In the schools, that was taken away. At school, instead of love, there was fear.

**Compassion:** Compassion is when you can feel for someone else. You don't turn away from them, you are kind. You understand they are going through something. Out on the land, you see that everywhere. Animals care for their young. They protect them. They stay close. In the schools, there was no compassion. If you were hurting, that did not matter. Instead of compassion, there was punishment.

**Respect:** Respect is something I learned from my dad. He would take me down to the river and show me how to be quiet around the beavers. He said, you don't disturb them. You let them bond with their young. That is respect — for animals, for people, for all things. In the schools, respect was not taught. It was replaced with control. At school, instead of respect, there was control.

**Courage:** Courage is not about being loud. It is about enduring. It is about getting through something when you are afraid. As children, we had to find that courage just to get through each day. But that is not how it is supposed to be. Courage is meant to help you grow, not just survive. At school, instead of true courage, we were made to feel small.

**Forgiveness:** Forgiveness is something you come to understand later in life. It is not easy. You carry a lot of hurt. But if you hold onto it, it stays inside you. Forgiveness is not saying what happened was right. It is letting go so you can heal. Instead of forgiveness, at school there was shame.

**Humility and not being selfish:** Not being selfish means you think about others, not just yourself. You share. You help where you can, in a humble way. That is how community works. Everyone looks after one another. In the schools, it was the opposite. It was about power and control, not caring for each other. Instead of selflessness, there was power over others.

**Wisdom, Knowledge, Truth and Honesty:** Wisdom comes from listening. From the land, from your parents, from your Elders. It is not something you are given all at once. It grows over time. When that knowledge is broken, it takes time to find your way back. But truth of the knowledge is still there. Just like those stars. At the school, instead of truth, there was silence.

There is a deep and wrenching sadness when our principles are not honoured. You can feel it. Not just in yourself, but in families, in communities. Something was missing when those teachings were taken away from us, it affects how we grow up. It affects how we see ourselves, and how we treat others. But those teachings were never gone completely. They are still there. Our parents carried them. The land still carries them. The stars still carry them. It takes time to come back to that. To remember who you are. To live those teachings again.

That is what we are doing now. May the Seven Sacred Gifts continue to guide us.

## Healing the Hurt

*I present a poem by my friend and colleague. KC*

Diane Bird

Memories, good and bad of
Indian Residential School
Where I learned to be tough
To stand up for myself
To cry silently where no one can see
To eat burnt lump porridge
To join track and field training
just to have bacon and eggs
To work in the kitchen
So I could steal food we couldn't have
To want to be loved so desperately...
And yet
I had a bed, food and clothing
I had good friends
I learned the 3-Rs
I learned responsibility
I learned not all teachers are bad
I chose to stay at the school
One and a half years
On summer and special holidays
Because my home life was rotten
Today, I reflect on past days
My higher power intervened
To save me for today
To teach my ways to others
That anything is possible.

## The Fist Fight

Told by Keith Chiefmoon
Transcribed by Lorene Shyba

My dad would often say to us kids, "When you make a mistake, you learn from that mistake." Most lessons come easy, but some get learned the hard way. Father DeWolfe, the principal at St. Paul's Anglican Residential School, discovered that when he tried to stop my father from taking us home for the weekend. What followed taught me something too: sometimes a person has to stand up against bad behaviour, no matter what.

When my brothers and I were sent to residential school, my parents had a really hard time with that. My mother cried when I had to go and that made me afraid. She had been at residential school too, so she knew what was coming. We were Catholic, so to say, but my family respected more the traditional ways. My dad, mother and grandparents were all active ceremonialists.

So, when I started school at six years old, I didn't speak English very well. We tried our best to understand what the nuns or the priests were telling us and would listen to the best of our capabilities but when we didn't respond to a question, they would take a stick and smack us across the head. As a result of all this, my hearing was damaged. Or they would grab us by the ear or hair and yank us in a violent way. That was the whole idea — they called it coming into civilization. How could they call this civilization? Instead, our environment was based on trauma and fear. How were we supposed to learn?

The first time my father stood up to the priest Father DeWolfe was when he insisted, "I will pick up my kids from school on the weekends. On Friday nights I will come and get them." That was his firm condition. So, on the weekends we would enjoy our time at home. We were happy out with Dad in nature and playing with each other.

But one Friday night later in the year, dad showed up to pick us up and there was a big confrontation. Father DeWolfe said to us, "You guys aren't going anywhere anymore, you're staying here." Even though dad was waiting, Father DeWolfe made us stay put in the school. We hid behind the door and soon could hear a bunch of scuffling and yelling going on outside.

Little did we know, but while this scuffling and yelling was going on, there were older kids watching out the window from the second floor at what was going on in front of the school between my dad and Father DeWolfe. One of these guys was Everett Soop, who became the famous cartoonist. He was with the other kids looking out the window and he watched the whole thing.

Everett later pulled me aside and said he wanted to share a story. He started out by saying, "Your dad is my hero." At the time, I thought he might be trying to make fun of my dad. But he said, "No, no, no, listen to me, I have a story about why he is really my hero. He is my hero because he is the only person who I saw take a serious stand against that priest."

By then I was interested in what Everett had to say. He continued, "I thought, oh my goodness, now your dad's going to get beat up by this guy, but your dad is tough. Your dad got really angry and grabbed that priest, got on top of him and rolled with him down the stairs and out onto the lawn. I was looking out the window and there was your dad, swinging at the priest, going toe to toe with him."

Then Everett laughed and so did I. I felt so proud of my dad at that moment, standing up to Father DeWolfe. Of course, these were all the scuffling and yelling noises we heard as we crouched behind the school door, scared as we were.

Everett finished up his testimony by saying, "Then your dad grabbed Father DeWolfe by his collar and spun him around. The priest staggered back, but your dad threw him up in the air and flipped him with his hip right onto the ground. I was just in awe. They were really going at it."

It was then that my brothers and I escaped from the school and made a beeline to dad's vehicle. As we were running to the car, Father DeWolfe tried to pull me back in the school by tugging my hair but I broke loose. That's when Dad strode over to the car, opened the car door and yelled to us, "Get in. Hurry up. Let's go!" and we all jumped in.

So, while we were trapped in the school, Everett was up in the second-story window watching the fight. Everett confirmed everything. All we knew at the time is that dad got his way and we were speeding away in the car for the weekend after all. The bond of our dad being our protector filled the air and he took us home.

When we got home, we greeted our mother and she gave us hugs and held us. I could still feel the fear and trauma rising up inside me, but she said, "It's okay, you're home now. Grab something to eat and then you can go outside and play." Later, we heard our parents talking quietly about how it was only a matter of time before the RCMP and the Indian Agent would come and take us back. But my dad dug in and refused to back down.

Residential schools were built on punishment and fear, but my father taught us that courage mattered more. He always said, "When you make a mistake, you learn from that mistake," and Father DeWolfe learned that lesson the hard way. I learned something too: sometimes you have to stand up to people who misuse power.

We never went back to St. Paul's instead we were sent to St. Mary's Catholic Residential School, but that's another story.

# EVERETT SOOP

My uncle Everett "Buno" Soop was a Kainai artist, political cartoonist, and social justice advocate from the Blood Reserve in southern Alberta, where I hail from as well. He was loved and well respected by his family and peers, drawing in people in all walks of life with his one in a million personality. Having been diagnosed with both muscular dystrophy and diabetes at an early stage in life, he chose to fight back, rather than give in, thru his meticulous style of artistry.

He was a Survivor of St. Paul's Anglican Residential School, and living with muscular dystrophy from a young age, he used humour and fearless observation to confront racism, colonialism, and the treatment of Indigenous people and people with disabilities. His cartoons remain powerful works of witness, critique, and courage. Everett died in 2001.

Everett was also an advocate of the always-present racial tensions between the First Nations Peoples and the Canadian government. Utilizing a mixture of art and humour, he created numerous works of cartoons, the context usually highlighting the ups and downs of reserve life, government corruption and racism.

Everett "Uncle Buno" died in 2001. My family including mom Crystal Many Fingers and sister Patricia Soop are pleased to see his work included in this book.

— *Alex Soop, author of* Midnight Storm Moonless Sky and Whistle at Night and They Will Come

---

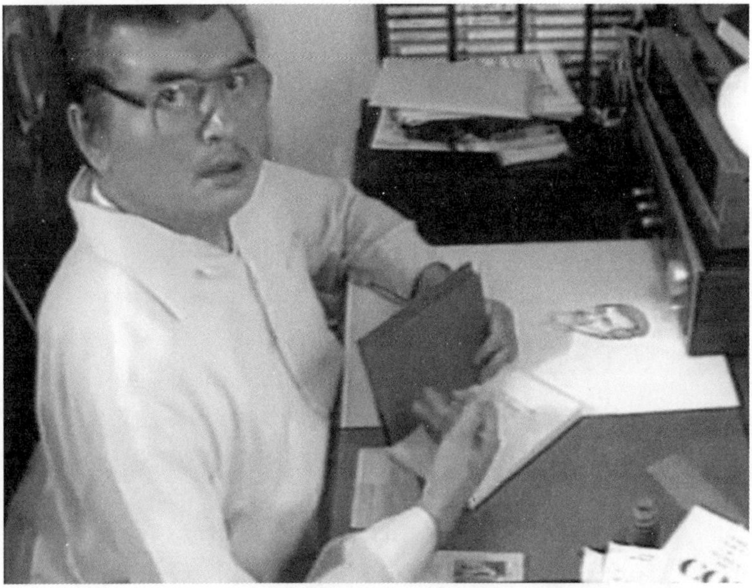

"Everett encouraged humour as good medicine. In our encounters at residential schools, that's what kept us going. We used humour as a way of releasing the trauma. — *Keith Chiefmoon*

"Everett's spirit is with us along with the spirits of those who never made it back home."
— *Eugene Arcand*

"One of most respected, controversial, and despised writers and cartoonist in his field."
— *Hugh Dempsey*

"[Everett] has joined the ranks of all great cartoonists who have traditionally bit the hand that nourished them." — *Pierre Berton*

## SCHOOL DAYS

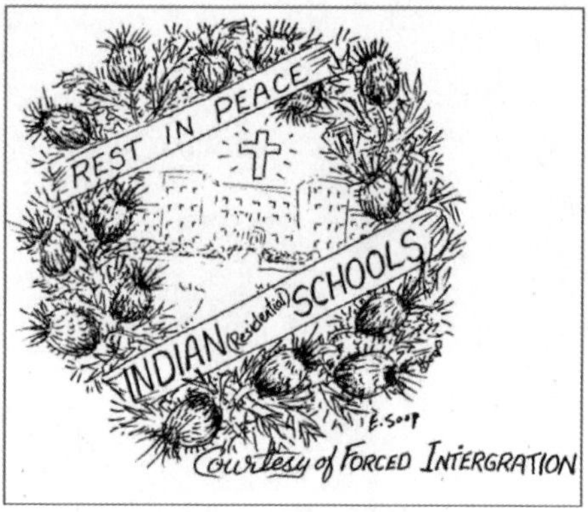


As you walk down its empty hallways there is nothing, nothing but silence. Only your footsteps echo throughout the building as if trying to be everywhere at once to revive the past. St. Paul's Residential School lies solemnly as though it had passed away to join Archdeacon Middleton, the man who was most responsible for building the school's grand tradition.

My mind often dwells for hours on those days that are still so vivid in my mind. Running away, getting a strapping, breathing, getting a strapping, expressing my sense of humour, getting a strapping. It didn't matter what I did; somehow I always ended up getting a strapping, whipping, lashing, or my hairline pulled up. Ears twisted. Slapped in the head, or maybe a full nelson by the supervisors, teachers, principal, or whatever. If you behaved and did as you were told you didn't fare any better because your peers nearly always administered the licking...

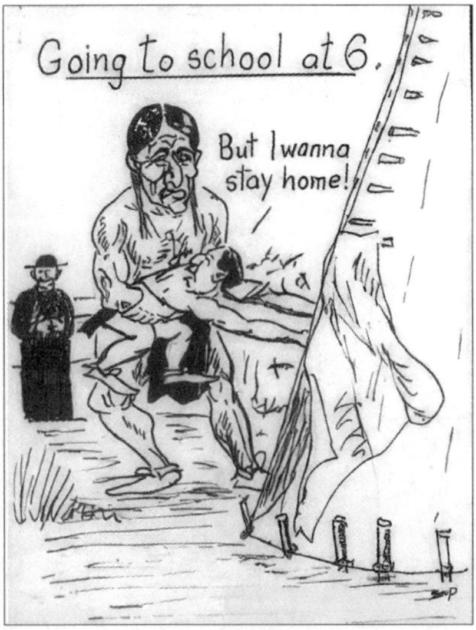


These are Archdeacon Middleton's "Home" rules:

- Do as you are told and do it immediately. A quick response to all bells is required.
- Parade in front of the Home before going to school, church or meals.
- Any windows or furniture broken will be charged to your ''Treaty'' money.
- No boy is allowed to leave Home school grounds without permission.
- Saturday afternoon is a holiday, any misbehavior on your part will cause you to lose it.
- Hats are to be worn outside and not inside the Home.

It is a good thing these brutal and violent institutions have ended, because the only good that they did was prepare you for the penal institutions.

Originally published in *Kainai News,* August 31, 1976

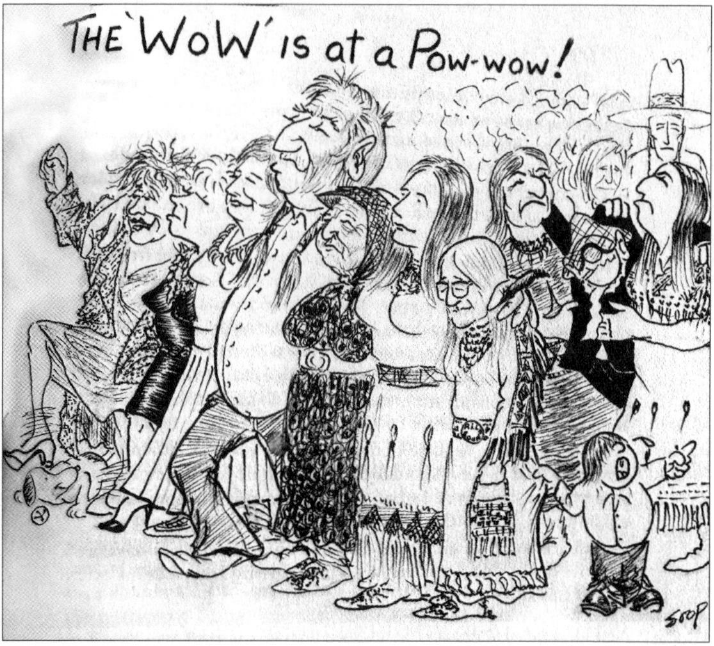
THE 'WOW' IS at a Pow-wow!
SOOP

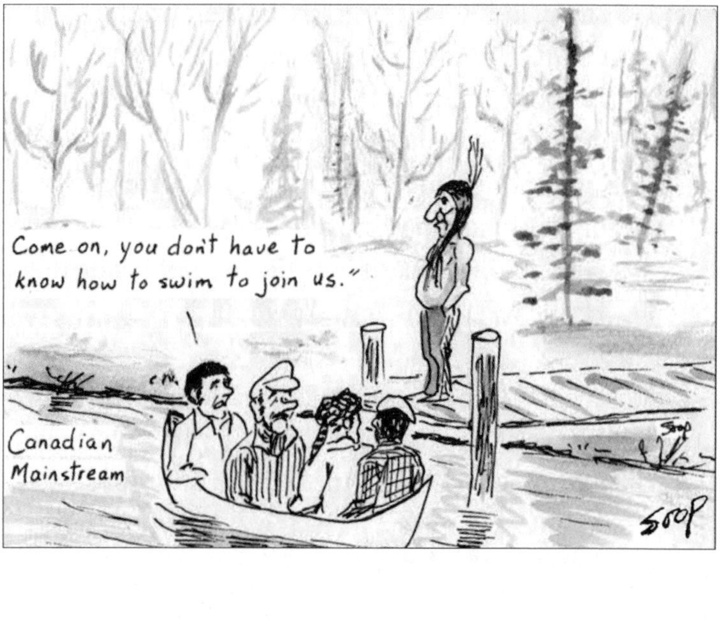
Come on, you don't have to know how to swim to join us."
Canadian Mainstream
SOOP

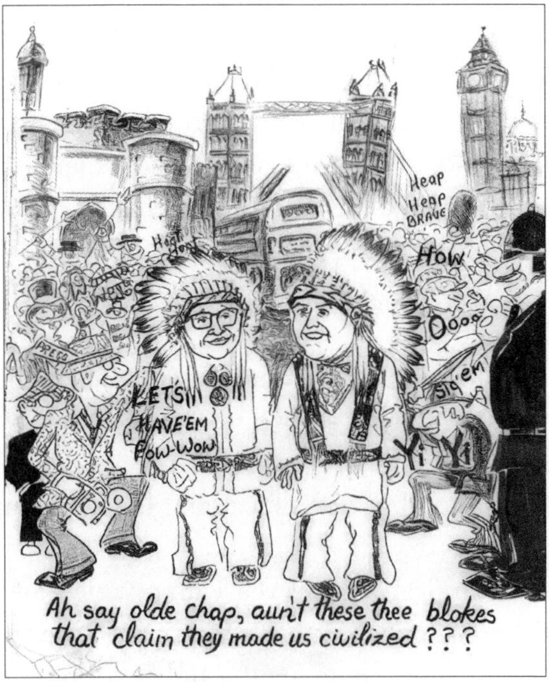
Heap
Heap
BRAVE
HOW
Oooo
Sic'em
Yi Yi
LET'S
HAVE'EM
POW-WOW
Ah say olde chap, aun't these thee blokes
that claim they made us civilized???

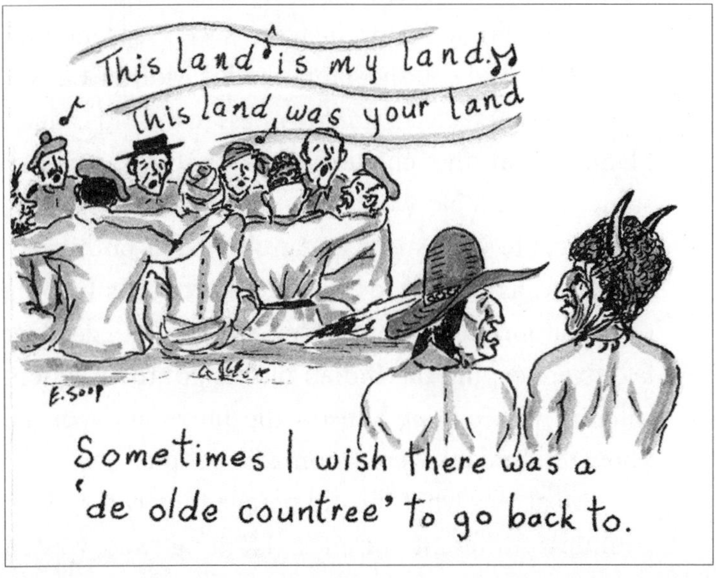
This land is my land
This land was your land
E. Soop
Sometimes I wish there was a
'de olde countree' to go back to.

## YOU ARE WHAT YOU EAT

Canadians eat the same as Americans, only in separate dishes. Of course, the cowboys eat pork and beans! And all this time, you thought that it was the horse that made the noise when it bucks. As you see, people are what they eat.

Now, you ask, what is the Indian like then? This is what he eats:

Guts for courage, but if he got too lazy, his guts usually became all hung out. The bear gave him the courage to claw away at chief and council. He was also very fond of dried meat and I'm sure you have noticed his dry sense of humour.

Pemmican was served with a variety of plants and herbs for seasoning. Pemmican lasted a long time which accounts for the Indian's long life if he survived infancy. Naturally he was well seasoned for all seasons and solidly planted to his Mother Earth.

If you detected a stubbornness in the old Indian, blame it on the chokecherries that he crushed, stones and all. No wonder he, at times, felt crushed and became very silent and stubborn at both ends. However, as an antidote he had a generous helping of saskatoon berry soup. This broth is an excellent laxative, keeping the Indian on the go; the frequent calls of nature kept him on the move and you all know the Indians were a nomadic people.

Meat was what the old people mostly ate, from countless different animals. Nothing was wasted

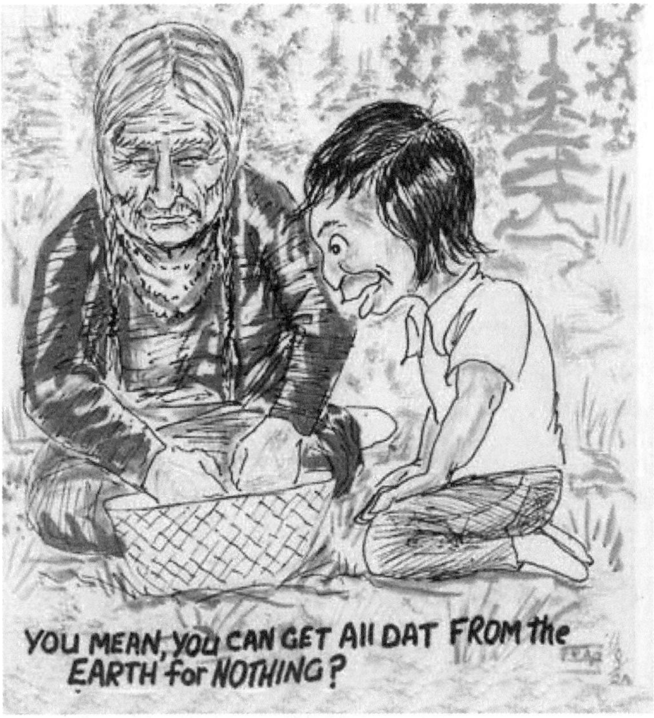


from what they killed. A real delicacy for those with big mouths was the tongue, while another delicacy was the moose's big nose which was usually devoured by the nosy people.

The deer is largely responsible for the natives' gentle nature, but those that were easily annoyed and often went berserk and charged into a fit of rage, were usually advised to avoid moose meat.

As for myself, I was usually the last to help myself to the much-loved saskatoon berry soup and by that time, all that was left was the bitter roots that were cooked with the berries.

Originally published in *Kainai News,* May 20, 1977

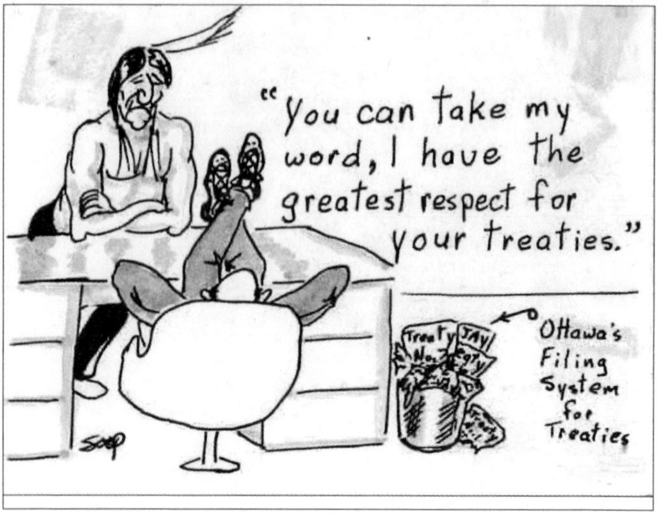
"You can take my word, I have the greatest respect for your treaties."
Ottawa's Filing System for Treaties
Soop

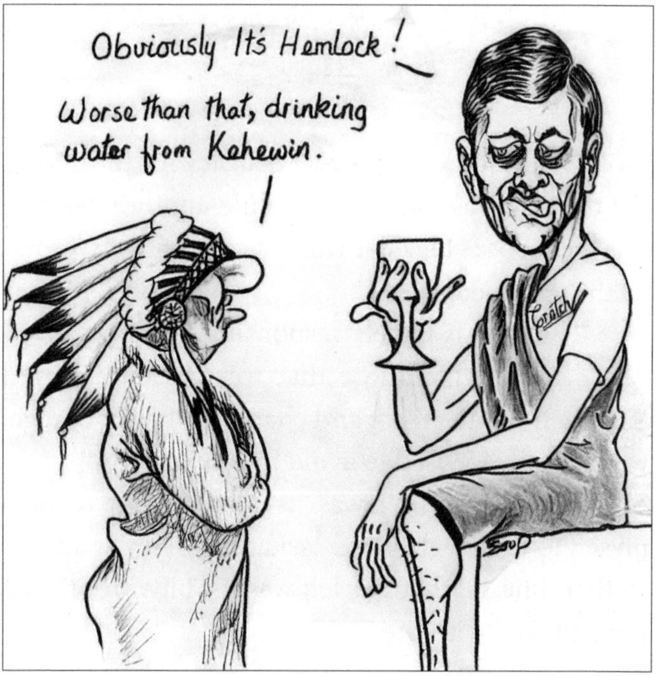
Obviously It's Hemlock!
Worse than that, drinking water from Kehewin.
Soop

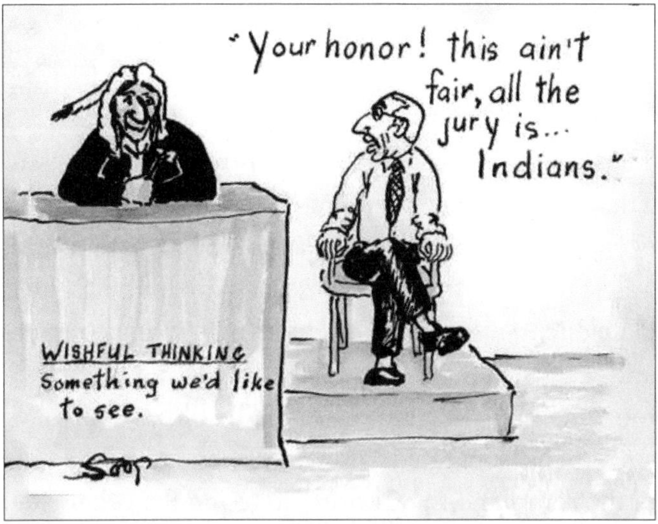
"Your honor! this ain't fair, all the jury is... Indians."
WISHFUL THINKING
Something we'd like to see.
Soop

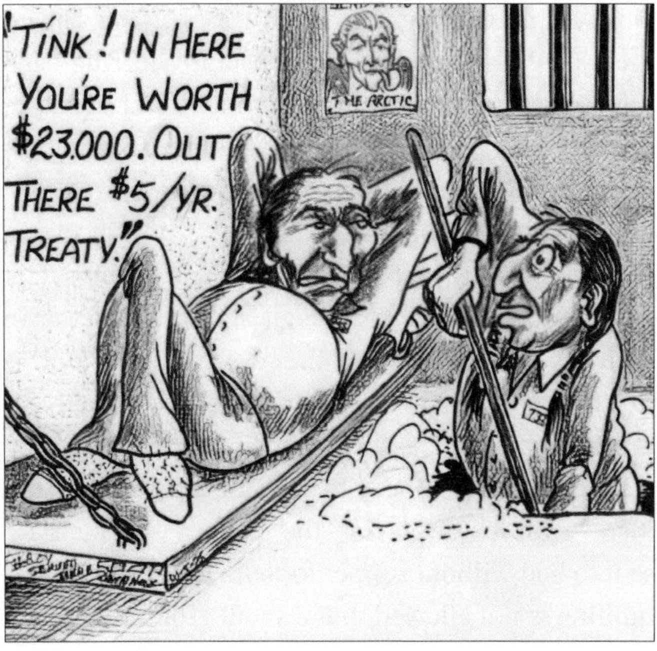
"TINK! IN HERE YOU'RE WORTH $23.000. OUT THERE $5/YR. TREATY."
THE ARCTIC

## A LETTER FROM PARADISE

Excerpt from A Letter From Paradise

Those that are a real disgrace are the politicians. They are still trying to make demands and run everything up here [in Paradise waiting room]. Latest talks centre around melting down the Golden Gate due to inflation and replacing it with a concrete and steel structure with a glass revolving door. Not too long ago they almost came to blows, but have since been separated with the Liberals on one side of the room and the Conservatives on the other side. In the middle are some NDP's who usually side with whoever is winning. However, this puts no end to their meddling as they are constantly jeering each other with the most atrocious profanities. I hear that in another part of the room the same is going on with Democrats and Republicans.

The only one that equals the politicians in boredom are the cowboys and their endless talk about rodeo. There is enough stock to partake in their favourite event, but they'd rather talk. Golf is just about being put to an end. Although there are miles of green grass, the golfers' swearing is causing a lot of embarrassment to the saints, especially the men of the cloth playing the game. Fishermen are sent to bed without supper for telling fish stories and hunting is not allowed, but a small group of hunters

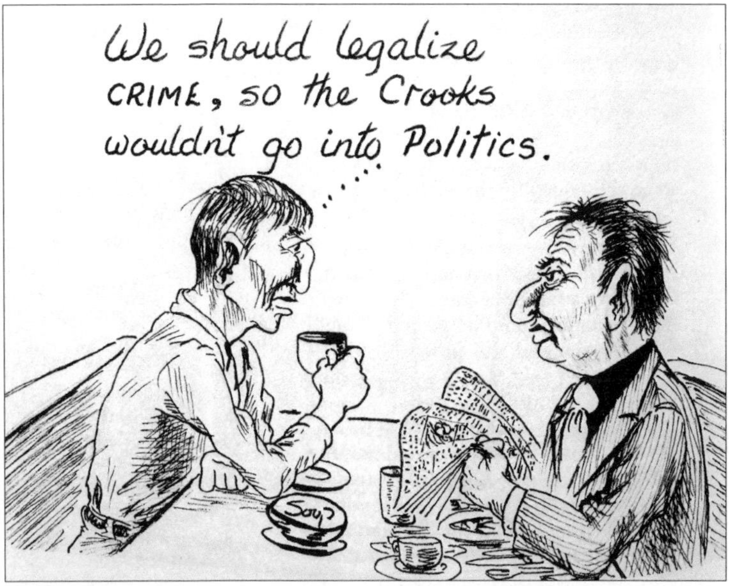


are threatening to go to the Happy Hunting Grounds and slaughter all the game.

I saw some of the Chiefs and Councillors from the "Grounds" trying to negotiate part of the Happy Hunting Grounds in exchange for more power, as well as to double their rations. However, the talk seem to be at a stalemate now, and already your trusty and honourable leaders at the Happy Hunting Grounds are planning a feasibility study trip to Hell to look at their most efficient heating system down there. Personally, I hope they don't come back as they will only be brainwashed by the Devil and all those Indian Affairs workers down there.

Originally published in *Kainai News*, April 1980

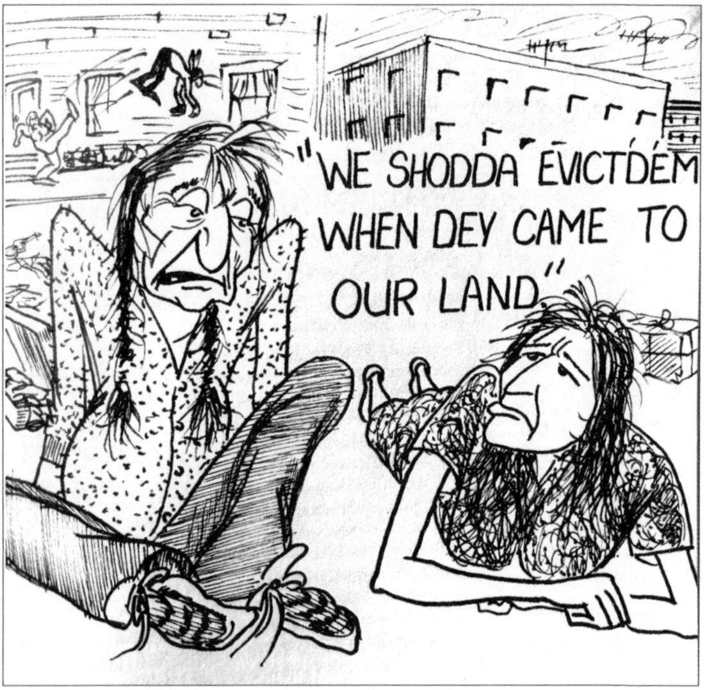
"WE SHODDA EVICTDEM WHEN DEY CAME TO OUR LAND."

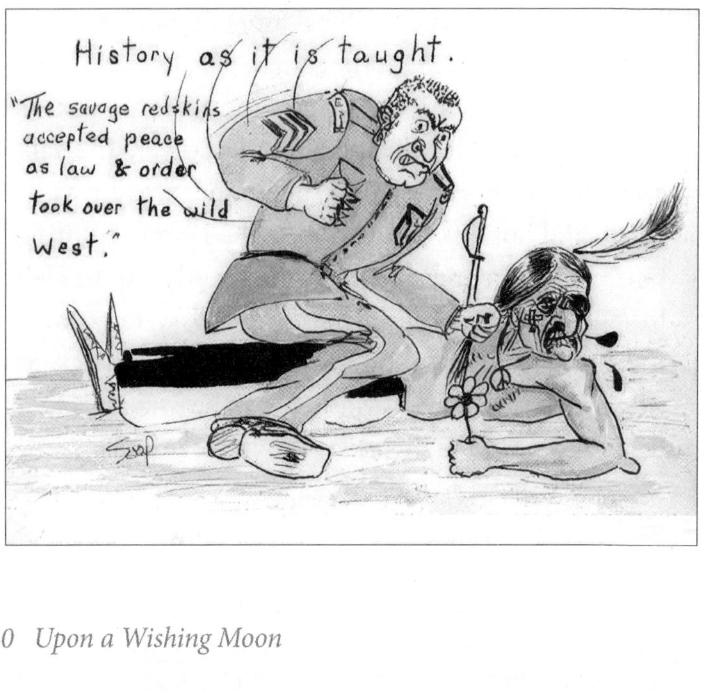
History as it is taught.
"The savage redskins accepted peace as law & order took over the wild West."

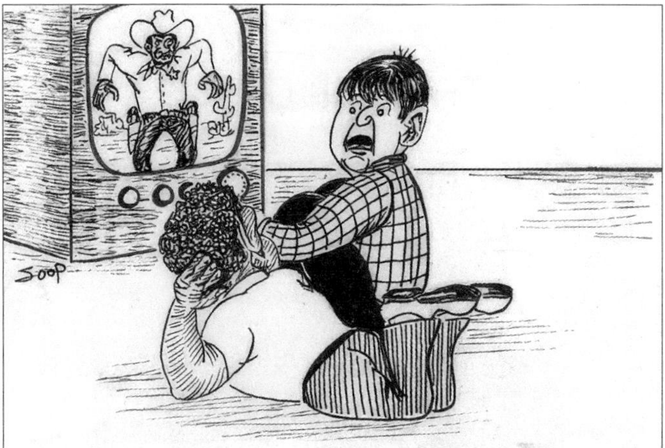


"Do you think us Indians will ever get To be good guys?"

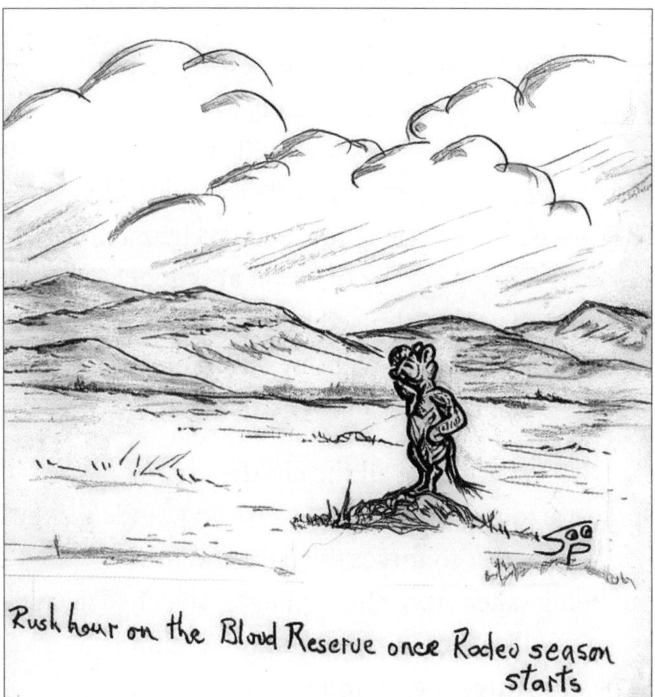


Rush hour on the Blood Reserve once Rodeo season starts

# *Afterword*

## "THE CHILDREN"

### CHIEF R. STACEY LAFORME

Where have all the children gone?
Some can be seen in the wrinkled face of age
Some can be found on the street homeless and alone
Some can be found in a battle with demons
Some have found their way back and teach and lead.

Some have gone to the spirit world.
Where I hope and pray that they
know only love and joy,
where they dance and sing in friendship.
They do not know the ignorance and hate of racism.
They were the ones left at school
The ones buried in the ground
The ones without a marker
The ones who never came home.

Where have all the children gone?
Some are found in their children and grandchildren
Never to forget the pain and hurt
of being taken from their villages, snatched away
Still running away from that school
still struggling to find where they belong.

Where have all the children gone?
They are still stolen from us by the jails,
the Children's Aid Societies, by a system that
never knew them or cared to learn.

Where have all the children gone?
It is a question from the past, a past that burdens
the present and casts doubt on the future.

Where have all the children gone?
A mantra from the past, a statement on the present
and a reminder for our future.

Where have all the children gone?
In the days to come, that mantra will change
Where have all the children gone? Home.
Where have all the children gone?
Home, home, home.
All are home.

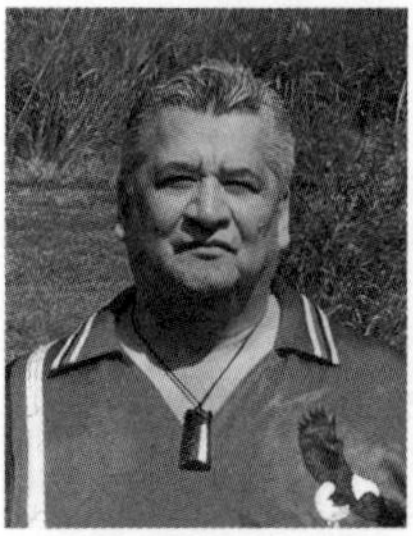

CHIEF R. STACEY LAFORME

*"We have told you our tales, we have shared our hearts and our spirits. Once you hear and understand it becomes a part a journey for your heart and spirit as well."*

Chief R. Stacey Laforme is a distinguished poet and storyteller from the Anishinaabe Mississaugas of the Credit First Nation.

# The Authors

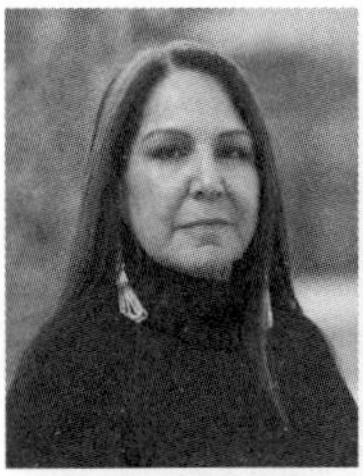
Stephanie Scott

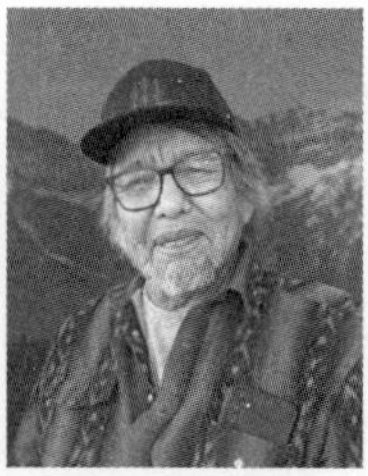
Dennis Saddleman

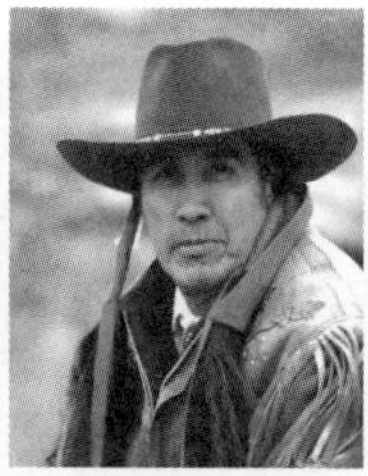
Dr. Antoine Mountain

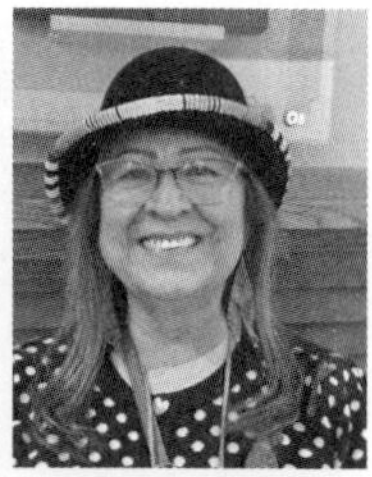
Dorene Bernard

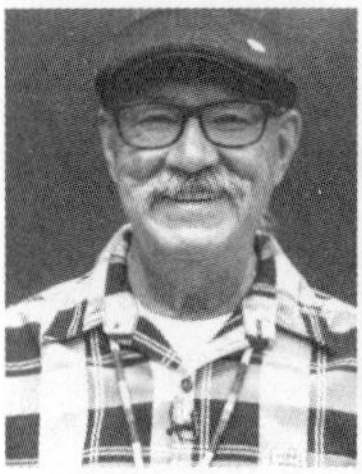
Eugene Arcand

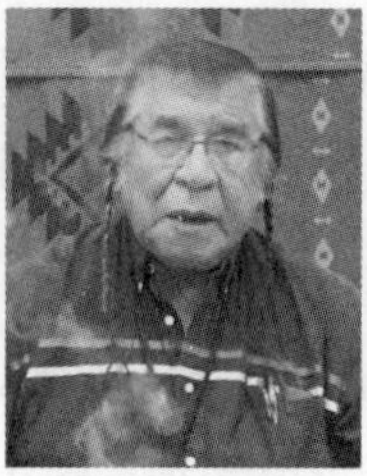
Keith Chiefmoon

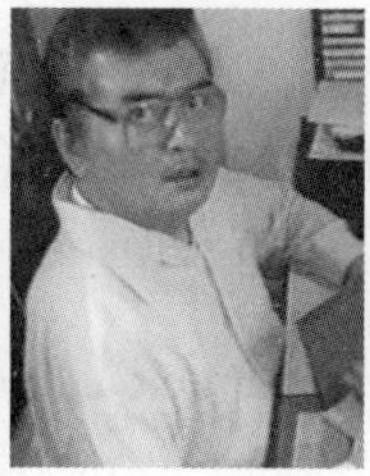
Everett Soop

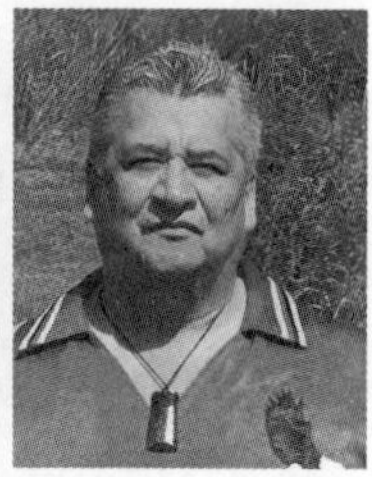
Chief Stacey Laforme

We are deeply grateful to the Survivors
and Supporters for sharing their
stories, poems, artwork, and wisdom.
It has been an honour to
bring these voices together.

Dr. Lorene M. Shyba,
Publisher
Crystal Many Fingers,
Indigenous Knowledge Keeper

Durvile & UpRoute